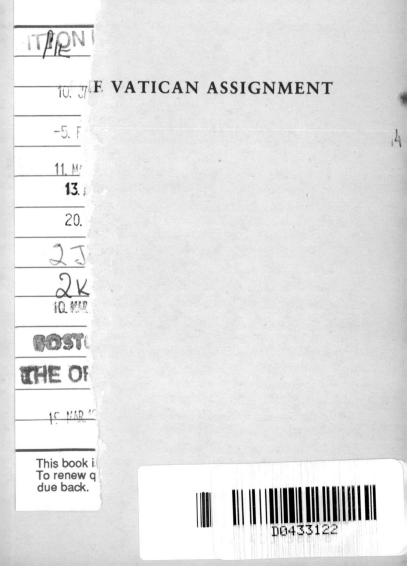

SOLDIER OF FORTUNE 3

THE VATICAN ASSIGNMENT

SOLDIER OF FORTUNE 3

THE VATICAN ASSIGNMENT

James Halliday

First published in Great Britain 1994
22 Books, Invicta House, Sir Thomas Longley Road,
Rochester, Kent

Copyright © 1994 by 22 Books

The moral right of the author has been asserted

A CIP catalogue record for this book is available from the
British Library

ISBN 1 898125 28 8

10 9 8 7 6 5 4 3 2 1

Typeset by Hewer Text Composition Services, Edinburgh
Printed in Great Britain by Cox and Wyman Limited, Reading

1

Jack Kelly swung his legs over the side of a deeply padded sun-lounger and stood up to stretch himself. Only his black swimming trunks broke the smoothly tanned surface of his firm body. He glanced at the other end of a thirty-metre pool where the source of his lavish, tax-free income for the past six months crouched beside a fountain, pulling the clothes off a skinny, bedraggled doll.

He made a face to himself and looked away, over a four-metre perimeter fence topped by razor-wire, down the rippling brown hills towards Cannes and the turquoise sea. He rolled his shoulder muscles and thrust his lower jaw into a smile that spread across his battered suntanned face. At least he had something worth spending his money on this evening. A few drinks with a beautiful woman, dinner somewhere small and intimate, and then, maybe, a moonlit boat trip to the islands.

The pleasurable thought was abruptly fractured by a shrill scream.

'*Jacques! Jacques! Ma poupée!*'

Kelly spun his head round and, almost simultaneously, started sprinting towards the four-year-old girl who leant over the rim of the fountain, wailing with frustration.

He reached the cascade, plunged his hand into the

few feet of bubbling warm water and fished out a Barbie doll clad only in elaborate underwear that had probably cost more than all his childhood clothing put together.

He shook it to get some of the water off and handed it to the girl. '*Voilà*,' he growled with a smile, not really wanting to blame the kid for the ignominy of the rescue he'd just performed.

'*Merci*,' the girl said, warmly enough.

'Béatrice?' An impatient young Englishwoman's voice reached them from a veranda above the pool. '*Qu'est-ce que tu as fait?* What happened?' The second question was addressed to Kelly.

Kelly looked up at the raw, red face of the girl's principal nanny. 'It's OK. Barbie was drowning,' he said in his leisurely Scouse drawl. 'I saved her and gave her the kiss of life.'

The nanny was scurrying down a flight of narrow stone steps now. Physical protection was Kelly's job; emotional protection was hers. She gave Kelly an exasperated look and ran beneath a pergola of purple bougainvillaea, across to the fountain. She knelt down beside the small child and put her arm around her.

Kelly shrugged and walked away, leaving the nanny to her ministrations. This will have to stop, he thought. He hadn't spent fifteen years perfecting techniques in survival, surveillance and close-quarters battle to rescue Barbie dolls.

A British Airways flight landed on the baking tarmac of Nice airport. A mixed bag of passengers stepped out of the plane, blinking in the midday August sun. Most of them were excited holiday-makers, naïve enough to think there was glamour to be found on the Côte d'Azur at this time of year. A few, who had read their papers for the whole flight like regulars on the London Underground, were businessmen in suits, bound for Nice or Monaco to occupy themselves with construction, scent, tourism or tax evasion.

A sleepy, now largely superfluous customs man looked perfunctorily at the stream of passengers claiming baggage and heading for taxis or greeters outside beneath the dusty palms. The only one to stir his interest – though he showed no visible reaction – was a tall Englishman in a quiet fawn suit. This passenger's short, dark hair was cut conventionally beneath a blemishless Lock's Panama. Around his neck, against a pale-blue shirt, was knotted a black and blue striped tie. His old-fashioned decorousness was in itself unusual in travellers on commercial flights into Nice these days, but it wasn't this that caught the attention of the French official. It was the pale-grey, almost motionless eyes – eyes with an opaque curtain just behind the pupil that permitted one-way vision only. He had seen eyes like this, in one or two men who had joined Customs after leaving the Deuxième REP. They were the eyes of a man trained to keep secrets very close; a man trained to kill, and to feel nothing while doing it.

The passenger glanced at the *douanier* and saw him looking. Unconsciously, the official straightened his back a little and acknowledged the Englishman with a polite nod. There was no cause to stop him. He had not waited for any luggage and carried only a slim, dark-brown briefcase. A man like that, the *douanier* knew, would not be wasting his time breaking petty or, for that matter, grievous customs regulations.

* * *

Sinking into the black leather upholstery of the white Mercedes which had been waiting for him outside the terminal building, ex-Major Piers Bowring relaxed. The French police didn't, on the whole, approve of his presence in their domain. There wasn't a lot they could do to prevent him being there, but given the chance, they were more than glad to waste his time asking questions and letting him know that they knew he was there.

The driver of the car, an ex-signaller who had served for eight years with the British Paras and four with the Royal Signals and Radar Establishment at Malvern, glanced over his shoulder as he swung the car on to the A8 towards Menton.

'Do you want to go to the villa first, boss?'

'Yes please, Terry.' Bowring's voice – concise, deceptively languid, Old Etonian – perfectly matched his clothing, though not his eyes. 'Have you got hold of Kelly yet?'

'In a manner of speaking.'

'Yes?'

'He took the bait. She's bringing him down tonight.'

'Michelle?'

Terry Haynes nodded with a grin which Bowring saw in the mirror.

'Are you still confident she's safe?' Bowring asked.

'Yeah. She's a career girl. So long as she never has anything big to sell, and you're paying her well, she'll be safe. So long as she thinks she's got prospects,' Terry added.

'And she still has no regular lover?'

'The day she has, sir, is the day to give her her cards.'

Bowring nodded. Michelle would need a good few

more wrinkles before she would require the emotional security of a committed lover. She was a spectacularly self-possessed woman; had she been less so, she would probably have been a movie star. She was certainly endowed with the acting skills which that might have called for.

'She's going to want more meaty jobs now, after Bosnia. How's her training going?'

'She can handle most small arms very effectively. She's getting good at CQB skills, and she could pass the RSRE operators' exams standing on her head; she speaks Italian, Russian, Serbo-Croat, German and Gulf Arabic, and she still looks like something off the cover of *Vogue*.'

Bowring nodded his head again but didn't speak. He looked out of the window at the parched, rocky foothills of the Alpes Maritimes, and awarded Kelly a minus for taking the bait so easily.

Kelly had agreed to meet the girl in a café on the main square in Vence. It had been her suggestion. She was the first French girl with whom he'd made any progress since he'd arrived at the Villa Diane to look after Béatrice Skiapoulos. Up until now, the local girls had ignored his advances and he'd written them off as snotty and arrogant. But this one hadn't made any pretence that she didn't fancy him.

He parked the Range Rover a couple of streets from the square and sauntered through the oblique early evening sunlight with a smile on his face; even the hint of a twinkle in his hard blue eyes.

What a turn up, he thought, finding a girl like that on the side of the road. Just standing there, two miles out of town, wearing a bikini top and a flimsy bit of chiffon wrapped around her waist. She hadn't told him why she was there. He'd asked her, but she'd just smiled. And she spoke brilliant English – better than his, really.

He strolled into the busy square, bought a newspaper and made his way unhurriedly across the square, crowded with busy shoppers and ambling tourists, to the café.

Although he was five minutes late, he hadn't expected her to be there before him. He found an empty table, sat down in a white plastic chair and ordered a pastis from a passing waiter. A glass of viscous yellow fluid and a jug of iced water were placed in front of him a few moments later. The waiter, almost as an afterthought before he turned to go, said: 'The young woman you are waiting for has telephoned. You're to meet her down in Nice, by the old port . . . Café Pelican.'

Kelly understood, despite the man's nasal Midi accent. He twitched with annoyance. In his experience, last-minute alterations to plans augured problems.

He watered his pastis, gulped back the glassful of now milky liquid and slapped a few coins on the table. Walking back to his car, he reminded himself that this wasn't a military operation; he was going to meet a girl – a very tasty-looking girl – at her suggestion. Who was he to complain if she'd had to change the venue.

Piers Bowring poured himself a deep measure of Stolichnaya with a splash of Perrier and carried it from the south-facing *salon* of the Villa Fleurie. He sat down at a table on a terrace beneath a pergola

6

and a wandering vine from which dangled bunches of small, dry, tasteless grapes. For a moment, like tens of thousands along that coast at that hour, he gazed down at a sea which glittered in the setting sun, and the little green hump of Cap Martin which protruded into it. But his cold grey eyes registered neither appreciation nor disapproval.

'Terry,' he called towards the house.

Haynes appeared at the french windows a few seconds later. 'Yes, boss?'

Bowring half-turned to speak over his shoulder. 'Bring Kelly's file out here, please.'

Bowring returned his gaze to the tumbling coast beneath him until the small cockney placed a yellow folder on the table in front of him. 'Sit down, Terry. You might as well go through this with me.'

Haynes drew up another wooden chair, so that they could look at the contents of the file together. Bowring was already familiar with them; he wouldn't have selected Kelly otherwise. But he wanted to make sure there wasn't any small detail he'd missed, and he wanted Haynes to know with whom he would be working.

From the assortment of regimental reports – which Bowring should never have seen – and from the letters, applications, citations and security assessments which he had managed to accumulate, a clear, if two-dimensional, picture of Jack Kelly had emerged.

Kelly had been born in 1955, in Toxteth, Liverpool, the second of five children. His parents, Eamonn and Mary Kelly, had arrived from Ireland with their parents in the mid-thirties. Nothing remarkable or derogatory was noted about them, beyond the fact that Eamonn Kelly had never earned enough money in the declining Liverpool docks to bring up their children. One could almost sense the relief they must have felt when Jack, having acquired half a dozen City and Guilds certificates at St Francis Xavier's RC secondary school, had announced that he was joining the Irish Guards on his eighteenth birthday.

What they might have felt when, five years later, he told them he had been accepted into 22 SAS, was more ambiguous. Both their families came from Co. Cavan, an area closely connected with Ulster across the border. No doubt their feelings were mixed when he married the non-Catholic daughter of a wealthy farmer on the Welsh borders whom he had met in a Hereford disco.

The records showed that Jack Kelly was an exceptional soldier, of the highest physical and mental resourcefulness. He came back from the Falklands in 1982 with a Military Medal for his sheer gall in carrying out surveillance operations, and after five years in the SAS he had been promoted to sergeant. He had an aptitude for disguise and languages, having acquired fluent Arabic – both classical and local spoken dialects – at the Royal Army Education Corps school at Beaconsfield by the time the short war against Saddam Hussein was waged. Here he served with distinction inside the Iraqi lines, pinpointing Saddam's mobile Scud missile-launchers. He lost one of his closest friends to an Iraqi land-mine, and returned to Hereford to find he'd lost his wife as well, to an up-and-coming tractor dealer.

At the end of '91, Kelly left the British Army, divorced and childless. At the time he was confident that his considerable skills and experience had a substantial value on the open market. But he balked at the idea of getting involved in other people's conflicts. To his growing disgust, he found most of the jobs on offer were concerned with mundane security, and providing what was known as 'close personal protection' to persons of sufficient political or financial clout to be considered targets.

Dull and frustrating, these jobs were nevertheless very well paid. After a year with a Saudi prince, during which he was under the mistaken impression that other, more varied duties would eventually be on offer, he had applied for a job in the team which looked after the toddler heiress to a billion-dollar Greek shipping empire. And that was only because, after Saudi, the locations sounded more attractive.

Though these reasons weren't specified in his file, Bowring knew, fairly accurately, what Kelly's motivation and aspirations had been. News of ex-SAS men was traded widely among their informal network, and Bowring had made it his business to keep up to date. He hadn't any doubt that Kelly and his extensive, hard-earned skills were utterly wasted in his current job, and that Kelly resented this.

'Looks like an all-rounder,' Haynes said.

'He is. Weapons, explosives, combat, plenty of covert experience. Dowson's got a job coming in where it looks as though I'll only be able to field three or four men.'

'What about the girl?'

Bowring nodded. 'I'll need her. She's got talents none of us could ever acquire.'

'Where did you find her?'

'I've known her since she was born. Hugue de Lassy — her father — was the best combat officer in the Deuxième REP I ever knew. We were working together in Lebanon when he got sniped by a militiaman in West Beirut. Her mother drove her car off the road in the Gorges du Tarn five years ago.' Bowring shrugged. 'I'd been a sort of uncle to her, and she'd always said she wanted to work with me. Of course, I ignored that and encouraged her to go to work in one of the international secretariats. She was always good at languages, then she got a degree in economics from the Sorbonne; she could have done anything she wanted. Last year, she came and saw me in England – she was working for Exxon – and told me she was ready to take on something a little more challenging.'

Terry Haynes was impressed. Michelle had been based at the villa with him for six months now, and she had never once mentioned this connection with their boss. That Bowring had never mentioned it before was to be expected.

'She's a hell of a girl,' Haynes nodded. 'Hard?' He sucked through his lips. 'She could give Tyson the brush-off and leave him wondering what hit him.'

'I take it she hasn't had cause to give you the brush off?'

'Course not. Even if it hadn't been standing orders, I don't think I'd have tried. I wouldn't have got anywhere. I don't think she's that interested in leg-over.'

'Just selective, I dare say. Let's hope Mr Kelly is quickly disabused of any ideas he might have about her interest in him.'

'D'you know him well, boss?'

'Yes. He was in my squadron in the Falklands, and he was the best of them. His marriage went wrong after the Gulf, but that'll have done him more good than harm – she couldn't take the pressure.

He'll suit this contract of Dowson's very well – if
we get it.'

'Who's the client this time?'

Bowring turned and looked at him for the first time
since he'd sat down. He lowered one brow in mild
censure. 'I'll let you know when it's in the bag.'

Monsignor Alfonso di Montefalco emerged from a
motorway tunnel – it must have been the hundredth
he'd passed through that day on his way up from
Rome – and blinked at the sun dropping behind
Mont Agel towards Monaco. He had enjoyed the
drive round the Ligurian coast, but he was tired now
and ready for a decent dinner, preferably with a good
bottle of wine.

He had been told that the English mercenary was an
exceptionally civilized example of his type; that was
partly why Montefalco had chosen to try him first.
In the one, discreet telephone conversation they had
had, Major Bowring's spoken Italian had certainly
impressed him. Archbishop O'Keane had stressed that
discretion was as important as efficacy in whoever he
instructed to do the job. Having listened to thousands
of confessions as a priest, Monsignor di Montefalco
had become an efficient judge of people's characters
from their voices. And this man had sounded more
than discreet.

The monsignor, if he had not been a cleric, would
very likely have become a politician. He was a clever,
good-looking man who possessed all the required
characteristics – not least ambition and a taste for
intrigue. It hadn't taken him long to work his way
up from a curacy in a poor Umbrian parish into the
bishop's office and thence to Rome, where his more

worldly predilections and personal vanity were less noticeable.

At forty-five, a year or two younger than the man he was coming to see, he still had a full head of fine, black hair and a trim figure. He liked to think that his sharp, handsome eyes, the colour of espresso, missed very little. Now they caught the signs for the exit down to Roquebrune and he throttled the big Fiat back to a hundred kilometres per hour. He took the slip-road over the autoroute and snaked down the hillside towards the glittering waters of the Côte d'Azur.

Haynes inspected the car and its driver through the security camera as the Fiat waited outside the villa's wrought-iron gates.

'Are you expecting some kind of vicar, boss?'

'Yes. Let him in and show him into the office.'

Haynes opened the electronic gates and the large car crept in and up the steep drive between the rows of cypress trees.

'I'll see him on his own,' said Bowring. 'Then I imagine he'll expect me to buy him dinner. I'll be back at eleven when Michelle gets here.'

His second in command nodded. 'Right. I'll take a run down to the end of the *cap*. And, boss, I was planning to take the girl out to the mountains tomorrow evening, to give her some practice with the new sniper and check out the laser sights system.'

'OK, but be discreet. They don't like us here and they don't need much of an excuse to chuck us out.'

'I'm always discreet. We'll have a couple of twelve-bores with us, to look as though we're lamping bunnies like the rest of the peasants.'

Bowring nodded philosophically. Without the vast army ranges of the Welsh hills at his disposal, he had to let his team use their initiative when it came to weapons training. 'Fine, and I'll want you back here later tonight when Kelly arrives with Michelle.'

'Right, boss.' Haynes gave a nod that acknowledged Bowring's position of command while at the same time asserting his own independence.

Jack Kelly squeezed the Range Rover between two Citroëns on the edge of the port in Nice and climbed out. There was the usual hubbub of fishermen, sailors, tourists and fun-seekers. Still warm but now dropping behind the castle on its rocky lump, the sun lit the upper storeys of the buildings on the opposite, east quay, and the lights of the bars and restaurants began to flicker on the oily water of the harbour.

Kelly sucked in a sharp, fishy smell which reminded him of the docks in Liverpool where he used to go as a small boy and dream of adventure and travel.

He spotted the Café Pelican and walked round to it with a rather different sort of adventure in mind.

The girl was sitting at a table outside on a chair of woven plastic. She looked at least as stunning as she had leaning back in his passenger seat a couple of days before. There was a cigarette between her lips and a packet of Marlboro on the table beside a bottle of local *rosé* and two glasses.

Kelly walked up to the table and grinned down at her.

'*Ça va?*' he said.

'OK,' she smiled back. 'I'm sorry I couldn't get to Vence. I was tied up down here.'

13

Her very slightly accented English made the idiom sound as if it were meant literally.

'Was that nice?' Kelly asked, then wished he hadn't.

The girl didn't answer.

Kelly pulled out another chair and sat down opposite her. She filled the second glass with pink wine and passed it to him. 'With the compliments of the proprietor,' she said.

'Why's that?'

'He's a friend of mine.'

Kelly had developed a taste for the *rosé* of the region and took a good gulp of it happily enough, but he resented the fact that he wasn't controlling this encounter in the way he would have liked.

'Do you come from here, then?'

She shook her head. 'No, but I'm living along the coast at Roquebrune.'

He realized he knew nothing about her. When they had talked in the car, it had been about him. He didn't even know her name.

'What's your name?' he asked with what he hoped was disarming directness.

'Michelle.'

'*Michelle, ma belle*,' Jack crooned in his appropriately Liverpudlian accent, '*sont les mots qui vont très bien ensemble.*'

Michelle smiled in a way that suggested this wasn't the first time she'd had those particular *mots* sung at her. 'When I was in England, they called me Micky.'

'Micky? That's absurd. What were you doing in England?'

'I was in the oil industry.'

This sounded sufficiently unlikely for Kelly to think it was probably true.

14

'What did you do in the oil business, then?'

'Nothing very interesting. That's why I don't now.'

'Well, what do you do now?'

Michelle smiled. 'I'll tell you sometime.'

Kelly shrugged. At least this suggested that there would be other meetings, and he understood that some people had the need for mystery. He was used to being secretive himself, but that was as a result of training rather than character. Many times his civilian friends, or his family, had asked: 'Where are you off to, then?' as he announced a forthcoming absence, and he would reply: 'I could tell you, but if I did, I'd have to kill you, so I won't.'

'You were a soldier, weren't you?' she asked.

He had no reason to deny it. 'Sure. Is it that obvious?'

'From the job you have now, looking after the little Skiapoulos. And because you are very fit.' She added this with a definite sense of appreciation.

'You spotted that, then?' Kelly said, pleased. At least there was some point in keeping in shape besides the need to rescue Barbie dolls. 'But how did you know about the Skiapoulos girl?'

Michelle shrugged. 'It wasn't very hard.'

No, Kelly thought, it wouldn't have been.

'Anyway, what about eating? What's the food like here?' He emptied the bottle into their glasses.

'Not bad, but there's a better place on the Boulevard Carnot.'

They finished their wine and walked a few hundred yards to the restaurant Michelle had suggested.

It was a warm, intimate place, serving classic

Niçoise food, and had an air about it that relaxed and softened.

Kelly and the girl talked, playing a game, shadow-boxing with the truth about each other. They had both travelled, and obviously shared a reluctance to put down roots. But Kelly learnt more about the girl from her eyes, face and gestures than anything she said – and he was impressed.

This was no bimbo, nothing like the girls who used to arrive in Hereford by the busload, ready to discard their underwear for any hard man with a tan, short-cropped hair and steely eyes who looked as though he was in the Regiment.

When they had finished eating, he hadn't, as he would normally have done, worked out a game plan, a series of initiatives that would lead her back to his bed; Michelle wasn't the sort of girl you led. And anyway, she pre-empted him.

'Come back up to the house where I live,' she said as he dropped a 500-franc note on the table. 'We can drink champagne and look at the moon,' she added with a shadow of a sardonic grin.

Kelly looked back at her, seeing the grin. She seemed to have reached some kind of decision. He couldn't guess what that decision was, but he made up his mind to take a chance.

Monsignor di Montefalco was sitting in a straight-backed armchair, fastidiously running his thumb and forefinger along the indistinct creases of his black trousers. Bowring had a chance to inspect him unseen for a moment as he silently walked into the room that they called the office. It looked more like the library of an Edwardian country house.

'Good evening, Monsignor.'

The cleric rose quickly and neatly to his feet and held out a hand in greeting. 'Major Bowring?'

Bowring nodded and closed the door behind him. 'Did you have a good journey?'

'Yes, thank you, though a very unsatisfactory lunch with the bishop in Lucca.'

'I have a table booked at the Chèvre d'Or in an hour's time.'

The Monsignor's eyes gleamed. He had not misjudged this man.

'But,' Bowring went on, 'I must ask you to change from you clerical garments, and we will have to converse there in Italian.'

Montefalco understood. He was proud of his crimson trimmings, but for dinner at the Chèvre d'Or, and for the sake of discretion, it was a small price to pay.

There was a quiet knock on the door.

'Come,' Bowring called.

A small, dark maid entered the room with a tray bearing coffee cups and a tall pot, which she placed on a table. When she had disappeared, Bowring said: 'I hope you don't mind coffee?'

'After four hours at the wheel, it is exactly what I need.'

Bowring poured, and indicated that they should sit opposite one another, before saying: 'So, Monsignor, I can't deny that I'm looking forward to hearing what you think we can do for you.'

The cleric looked back at him for a moment before he spoke. 'What, as a matter of curiosity, do you think it might be?'

'I really couldn't say, I'm afraid.'

'A man of your experience and practical knowledge of the world must surely be able to make an intelligent guess?'

'Of course, but that's not the same as knowing. And I'm not privy to the detail, or even the general thrust, of Vatican foreign policy, if there is such a thing.'

The cleric smiled. 'There most certainly is. But tell me your intelligent guess.'

'The Vatican is sending a pro-nuncio to Tel Aviv, and certain Islamic bodies are not best pleased.'

The Papal officer smiled, with a nod of encouragement. 'And?'

'And you're expecting a spot of trouble,' Bowring said with a slight display of impatience.

Montefalco noted this. 'Quite, quite,' he said quickly. 'More than a spot of trouble. Our legation in Damascus has received some information about a group of zealous who go by the name of Sufuf Allah – The Ranks of God.' He pursed his lips in distaste. 'These people plan to make a name for themselves by . . . neutralizing – as I think you say in your trade – His Holiness.'

Bowring nodded without expression.

'You are not surprised, or appalled?' the monsignor asked him.

'No,' Bowring said quietly. 'It's a while since I was surprised or appalled.'

Montefalco appeared to accept this, quite gladly. 'I'm told that you saw service fighting with Arabs against Arabs in Dhofar, so I presume you have no ideological problems in that direction?'

'I'd say that I was fighting for the interests of the free world against the deadening spread of communism.'

18

'And is that the only reason you did it?'

'No. I did it because I was good at it, and I enjoyed it.'

The cleric nodded, sadly pragmatic, 'Someone has to do these things. There is no doubt that God grants His blessings to the defenders of the free.'

Bowring allowed himself a small smile. 'Let's hope so.'

'Now, the very apogee of God's church on earth is under threat. It is not the first time, and it will not be the last. But if followers of Islam were to succeed in destroying our Pope in the current state of world tension, it would go a long way to encouraging militant Muslims everywhere, as well as depriving us of a great and good spiritual father.'

Bowring expressed no opinion on this; he had none to offer.

'Not only must we make sure that this plan does not succeed,' Montefalco went on, 'but we must also be sure that no one even hears of it. There are only two people in the Vatican who are aware of this current threat, myself and Archbishop O'Keane, who is head of security. Bishop Rappacioli, the Nuncio in Damascus, knows, and now you do too.'

Bowring nodded.

'His Holiness, as you may know, is making two foreign tours in the near future,' Montefalco went on. 'Three days in India at the end of this month followed by six days in Britain during September. Our information is that the attempt will be made on one of these tours. It is difficult to approach him armed in the Holy City.'

'Is it? With all those crowds and audiences?'

'Our Guardia Svizerra are not entirely decorative.'

'Then why aren't you briefing them on this job?'

'Major Bowring, they are good, well-trained soldiers, but quite frankly they are not remotely in the same league as men trained in, for example, Russia's Spetsnaz, Israel's Sayeret Matkalz, or the French Deuxième REP, or of course, your own 22 SAS, who still reign supreme, do they not?'

2

Out of habit, Kelly pushed the Range Rover to the limit through the chicanes and hairpins of the Grande Corniche. If the girl was scared or impressed, she didn't show it. When they reached the hillside village of Roquebrune, she directed him concisely to the house where she said she lived.

There was a tall, purposeful gate across the bottom of a steep drive which led up to a large, well-lit villa.

'I'll do the gate,' Michelle said. She jumped down from the vehicle and walked to a video entryphone set into one of the tall stone gateposts. By the time she was back in her seat, the gates had silently swung open. They were already starting to close as Kelly drove between them. He wondered again, but Michelle offered no explanation for the security surrounding the house.

She didn't speak until she was ushering him into a high, cool, tiled hall lit by a small chandelier. When the oak front door was closed behind him, she said: 'This villa belongs to my boss. I'll introduce you to him.'

She opened one of a pair of carved fruit-wood doors into an old-fashioned French *salon*.

Kelly followed her into the room, expecting the unexpected.

'Evening, Kelly.' The voice entered the room as the speaker stepped in through french windows which opened on to the glittering panorama of the coast below.

Kelly's surprise at seeing Bowring lasted only a fleeting moment. Major Piers Bowring had in the past provided him with enough mind-jarring surprises to have made him largely immune to them.

With barely perceptible hesitation, he answered: 'Evening, boss,' as if he had seen Bowring the day before.

'Drink?'

'Your messenger promised champagne.'

'Champagne it shall be. Nothing but the best for an ex-hero of H Squadron.' He walked across to a walnut cabinet which contained a fridge in its lower part. He took out a bottle of Louis Roederer Cristal Brut and filled two glasses, which he handed to Kelly and Michelle before splashing a long measure of Stolichnaya into a tumbler for himself.

Kelly took a drink of the mellow, bubbling liquid and erased from his mind a lot of the questions that had been nagging at him for the last few hours. It was almost a relief to have them answered, and he wasn't going to let the girl see his disappointment. Thank God, he thought, he hadn't succumbed to the temptation to proposition or pounce on her.

'Sit down, Jack,' said Bowring.

Kelly lowered himself into a deep armchair. Bowring walked behind a handsome maple writing table and sat down behind it. Michelle walked over to the window and remained standing.

Kelly had accepted the obvious fact that the girl had sought him out and brought him here under instructions. That didn't necessarily mean that there was no mileage to be got out of her — unless, of course, she was Bowring's girl. He stiffened slightly at the thought, and thanked his stars again that he hadn't made a fool of himself with her.

'So, how are you enjoying life at the moment?' Bowring asked.

'What do you think?' Kelly asked and tossed back another gulp of champagne.

'I imagine you're bored rigid and ready for a change. Michelle wouldn't have brought you here otherwise.'

Kelly nodded with a grin. He hadn't set eyes on Bowring for nearly ten years, but the man hadn't changed at all; perhaps a touch greyer of hair, but the eyes and voice were as sharp as ever. They'd been through plenty of shit together, he and Bowring, on the slopes of Mount Kent and in West Belfast – been through it, saved each other's lives a couple of times and come out the other side. He'd heard rumours that his old boss had set up in business but nobody seemed to know where.

'But the money's good. Have you got a better offer?'

'Maybe. You'll have to decide that for yourself, once I've made you the offer. But first I need to be sure what sort of condition you're in.' He was scrutinizing Kelly as he spoke. 'You look in good shape. Do you still run?'

'Yeah. Eight, ten miles, most days.'

'Could you still do the Long Drag across Pen-y-Fan inside twenty hours?'

'I could do it quicker now than I did at Selection.'

'What about weapons training?'

'I've kept it up, at least with small arms. I joined the gun club in Nice when I first got down here, and in Saudi they let me use their army ranges.'

'Gimpies, Stingers?'

Kelly looked surprised. You would only need a General Purpose Machine Gun or a hand-held SAM launcher in outright open combat. 'I'd need a bit of practice,' he admitted.

'And you're not worried about live targets?'

Kelly shrugged. 'You know what it's like. A target's a target.'

'OK. I'll want to have a look at you in action. We've got some L96s with laser sights and a few other bits of high-tech which you may not have used before.'

'But what's the job, boss?'

'Jobs,' Bowring said. 'I'm glad to say there's no shortage of work at the moment.'

Bowring stood and walked round to the centre of the room. 'I'll tell you more about it when we've both decided that we want to work together. For starters, are you prepared to undergo my short selection process?'

'How long's "short"?'

'A day or two. When is your next week off?'

'Starting Monday.'

'Fine. Come here then. And tell no one. If I want you, I'll want you right away, so you'll have to think up some reason. Our doctor can fix you up with a certified broken ankle if necessary.'

He held out a hand. Kelly stood and took it, realizing the interview was at an end.

'See you Monday, then – 0800.' Bowring nodded farewell and strode out of the room, closing the door on Kelly and Michelle.

The girl hadn't spoken since showing him into the office. Now she picked up the bottle of champagne and refilled their glasses. She lifted hers. 'Good luck,' she said.

Kelly walked over and looked out of the french windows on to the bay below. Slowly he turned back, looked at the girl and shook his head. Shit, she's lovely, he thought – and hard as fucking granite.

'Did he put you through selection?' he asked.

'Oh yes.'

'Is he your boyfriend?'

The girl smiled. 'He's my godfather, actually.'

Kelly couldn't imagine anyone seriously entrusting their offspring's spiritual guidance to Piers Bowring. On the other hand, Bowring had a lot to teach in other areas, if he chose to. Kelly wondered who the girl's father was, but he knew he'd asked enough questions for now.

'Right. Thanks for the drinks. I'm off.'

'Thank you for dinner,' she said, smiling back politely.

She opened the front door for him and watched him down the steps to the Range Rover.

'Good night, Sergeant,' she called softly.

Kelly didn't answer and climbed into his vehicle.

He roared down the drive, guessing that the gates would be open before he reached them. They were, and he spun out of the entrance on to the narrow road, heading towards the Grande Corniche, trying to sort out what the hell he was feeling.

The four days until the following Monday dragged like a prison sentence.

Kelly's tiny charge and her team of nannies were really beginning to get on his nerves. But he was a professional; he didn't let it show. He'd stood six months of it and another few days weren't going to kill him.

But he could hardly believe how turned on he was by the thought of getting back to some real action. He felt as if he had just been treading water, killing time since he had left the SAS.

It was a common syndrome.

They trained you up to the eyeballs; after fifteen years, you were a top man in the most élite regiment in the world's finest army. You didn't have anything to prove to anyone. But you became addicted to the adrenalin so that the gaps between action became unbearable, and when you left you found yourself facing a gap that threatened to last the rest of your life.

All the organizations who preyed on the men leaving the Regiment promised the earth: lots of money, travel, action. But it was all bullshit.

Close personal protection; sitting around for hours outside casinos or government offices, getting rigid with boredom until you began to hate the poor bastard you were supposed to be protecting. It might have been all right, as it was for a lot of his former colleagues, if he'd had a wife and children to worry about and pay for.

But all that had fallen apart for him. He would have liked children, he supposed, but he was bloody glad he'd never had one by Susan. Of course, his family thought he was mad. They thought he was wrong to have left her, despite the tractor dealer. They thought he could have got a highly paid, safe job with the police, or Customs and Excise. They didn't trust him any more, didn't know what to say to him when he came home tanned, with a pocketful of money. So he'd stopped going.

The Regiment had become his family, although he'd only discovered that after he'd left.

Since then, he'd forced himself to get used to being alone. He liked women and his ice-blue eyes and obvious independence had kept him supplied, but he liked them for the excitement of the chase, the chat, the buzz of the early stages of encounter. He didn't want women to know him well enough to see his moods or his loneliness.

And now Bowring was proposing that he should join a new family, and he wanted it and the action it promised. Clever bastard, Bowring.

Kelly didn't concern himself with how the major had known that he was ripe for recruitment. Of course, Bowring hadn't known for sure, but he'd sent the girl to check him out, and she'd taken him in.

He turned over in his big bed, in the large, airy room just down the corridor from the little billionairess and wasn't sorry at all that this was to be his last night in that room.

Monday was one of those rare, stormy days that whip down the Côte d'Azur in August, with a sharp, wet wind that blew down off the Alps to fill a vacuum in the atmosphere somewhere out beyond Corsica.

The change in the weather suited Kelly as he hurled his suitcase and a couple of bergens into the back of his Range Rover and blasted his horn at the sleepy gatekeeper of the Skiapoulos villa to let him out. He didn't want to be a second late for whatever selection course Bowring might have devised and drove through Vence as the market traders put the finishing touches to their stalls at half-past six.

* * *

The door of the villa was opened at eight o'clock by a man Kelly didn't know – a Londoner, judging from his accent.

'Morning, Mr Kelly. Have you left your keys in your vehicle?'

Kelly nodded.

'Good,' the little cockney said. 'Come in. I'm Terry Haynes.'

The weasel-faced man held out a hand with a cheerful grin. Kelly shook it and made an instant assessment. Definitely ex-services, definitely not ex-Regiment, but sound nonetheless.

'Morning,' said Kelly, appreciatively sniffing a whiff of strong coffee wafting into the hall. You didn't get any of that before Selection in Hereford in the old days.

It turned out that you didn't get any in Bowring's outfit either.

Haynes opened a concealed door in the painted panelled wall of the hall and beckoned Kelly to follow. The door opened on to a flight of narrow stone stairs which led down into a cellar.

'Shut the door firm behind you,' the cockney told Kelly and switched on half a dozen fluorescent lights.

The vast stone cellar appeared to have been cut right into the hillside, and had a number of tunnels hewn from the solid rock. The man-made walls on the south side were lined with metal Dexion shelving like any quartermaster's stores. On the shelves were stacked tidy row upon row of military gear: all-weather kit, clothing, communications equipment.

Haynes swiftly pulled out olive-green fatigues, a green ribbed pullover, Gore-tex jacket, heavyweight bergen, net scarf, torch, prismatic compass, water bottles and webbing belts to strap them to – everything the fully equipped SAS trooper might be expected to carry – except his weapons.

He dumped it all on a folding table in front of Kelly and grinned at the look of surprise on his face.

'I suppose you thought all our gear would by Yves St Laurent.'

'I was just wondering where it all came from.'

'You can buy most of this stuff if you know where to look. Have you brought your own boots?'

Kelly nodded. 'Yeah. What about a knife?'

'No knife. No shooters. No weapons of any sort, I'm afraid. But there'll be an L96 7.62mm waiting for you when you get to your last RV – just to make sure you can still hit a target.'

Kelly shrugged. It looked as though he was in for a good old-fashioned yomp. Evidently Bowring hadn't accepted Kelly's own assessment of his fitness or weapons skills.

This was confirmed when Haynes gleefully stuffed the bergen with fifty-five pounds of engineering bricks.

'Right,' Haynes said, looking at his watch. 'You've got less than an hour to get to the start line and cross it fully loaded. And eight hours to get to the finish. Your maps and grid refs are already in your vehicle.'

'What? In my own Range Rover?'

'Sorry, mate. No company cars supplied till you're on the payroll. Don't worry. It's all clean roads up to the start, but you'll have to give it a bit of welly. I'll get your rations and fill your bottles while you're changing.'

Haynes disappeared into a room at the end of a row of shelves, and Kelly mechanically set about pulling on the familiar kit. He didn't know yet where he was headed, but it was a fair guess that it would be high ground. What was harder to judge was what the weather would be like by the time he got there. But then, he could decide if he needed the Gore-tex when he reached the start.

As Kelly buckled on his belt, Haynes came back with two water bottles and a handful of dry rations, – enough for a short day's yomp – and stuffed them into the bergen on top of the bricks.

Haynes looked at his watch again. 'Right. It's 0815. You've got to cross the start line at 0900 so you'd better piss off – out the back way.' He jerked a thumb towards one of the tunnels hewn in the rock-face. 'That takes you up and drops you on to the back road to the village. You'll find your vehicle parked directly outside. Don't worry about locking the door, we'll do that, but don't let anyone see you come out. Best of luck.'

'Thanks.' Kelly felt like an eighteen-year-old rookie as he entered the unlit tunnel. He unhooked his torch and followed the passage round a bend, up a steep flight of fifty steps until he reached a heavy, double-bolted iron door. He drew back the bolts and the door swung silently and smoothly towards him, letting in daylight filtered through a curtain of scrub oak and dangling vegetation.

He pulled the door to behind him and carefully edged his head forward through the leaves until he had a clear view of what lay beyond. He was on one side of a shallow cutting through which ran a narrow lane. Directly in front of him, six feet below, was the roof of his Range Rover parked in a passing place. There were no houses or people visible for fifty or sixty yards in either direction. A small Citroën van with corrugated sides laboured up the hill towards him, passed him and carried on east, towards the village, Kelly reckoned. He waited a few seconds after it was out of sight and hearing, to listen for any more approaching vehicles or pedestrians. Satisfied there were none, he parted the branches in front of him and scrambled down the bank.

The left-hand-drive Range Rover was facing down the hill, with the driver's door closest to him. He heaved off the bergen and removed his loaded belt and opened the door to chuck them in, then climbed in himself. The keys were in the ignition, and there were two maps folded on the passenger seat. Kelly switched on the engine; it was still warm. He wondered vaguely who had brought it round, and realized he hadn't a clue how many people Bowring employed at this place. But perhaps the girl knew; maybe she was watching him even now.

Then he put the Range Rover into gear and shot off down the hill. The lane took a couple of hairpins and came out on the Moyenne Corniche. He drove a hundred yards along the main road until he reached a safe pull-in, and began to study the maps. On the first were written two grid references marked 'start' and 'finish'.

Within seconds Kelly identified the start just above the village of Sospel, due north from where he was, on the edge of the Mercantour National Park, well up in the Alpes Maritimes. He checked the route – about six miles along the autoroute, then twenty miles of switchback road up the Carei valley. He quickly memorized the route and pulled off again with a scattering of wet gravel.

The rain had stopped for the moment, but the wind kept coming, and the sky hadn't cleared. Within five minutes Kelly was heading east on the fast lane of the A8 in a spray of surface water.

In another five minutes he was pulling off the highway on to the *route départementale* that led up into the foothills. He flicked the transmission to four-wheel drive and gave every ounce of his concentration to climbing that road as fast as was humanly and mechanically possible.

Kelly parked in a small, quiet square in Sospel at 0854 hours. The rain had been beating down for the last few miles of the journey, and the clouds up ahead didn't look forgiving. He decided to keep the Gore-tex.

He climbed out, pulled out the bergen and belt, slotted the map into a perspex holder, then, after locking the car, heaved the rucksack on to his back and set off for the start.

He saw no sign of anyone watching or monitoring him at the first reference point. But then he hadn't expected to. He shrugged his shoulders, hoisted the bergen a little higher on his shoulders and headed into the wind.

The first two miles were fairly easy going along a rutted track, but he knew he would have to strike off it, and over the shoulder of the hill to pick up the intermediate grid refs he'd been given.

The straps of his bergen had settled into his shoulders and he had found a rhythm in his walk – a good, steady three miles an hour, he judged. He pulled a Mars bar from his smock and munched it as he walked, and asked himself what the hell a man of his age and experience was doing playing at trainee soldiers.

There was a time when he might have written off this bogus 'selection' yomp as a load of bollocks. But somehow he couldn't associate that with Major Piers Bowring. The major was a serious man and always had been.

Bowring had been on his second tour with the Regiment when Kelly had first come across him. He already had the reputation from his first tour as a troop commander of not being quite like the other officers. Out in Dhofar, as a twenty-three-year-old 'baby Rupert', he had shown as much guts and tactical instinct as any hardened old sergeant-major, and his reputation was well established by the time he came back a few years later from his parent regiment, the 17th/21st Lancers, to command his own squadron.

The troopers and NCOs of 22 SAS enjoyed a tradition of easy relationships with their officers. It was one appropriate to the kind of operations in which they were engaged, where every man was equally exposed to danger and equally in need of the mutual support they could give one another.

But Bowring had always been a bit aloof. He made no pretence of being interested in drinking or fraternizing with his troop or his squadron and clearly disapproved of the idea of currying popularity with his men. He expected them to accept him for what he was, and what he had done.

Where they would be ogling *Penthouse* or *Playboy*, he would be reading *Newsweek* or Trollope or A.J.P. Taylor.

When he had rejoined the SAS, he had insisted, quite

unnecessarily, on undergoing a physical Selection all over again, along with a bunch of aspiring recruits. On a sixty-kilometre slog across the Brecons in mid-January, he had romped home with a sixty-pound load on his back, an hour before the next finisher.

In the Falklands, he'd shown supreme skill and tenacity in placing his squadron in critical observation posts, sometimes a mere hundred yards from enemy positions. He had personally led the raid on an airfield on East Falkland, destroying six Pucaras, three helicopters and twenty-eight Argentinians with the loss of only one of his own men.

Yet after the Falklands, something had gone wrong with Bowring's career. No one Kelly had ever asked seemed to know what had happened, but abruptly in the summer of 1985, Bowring had resigned his commission, and gone. Thenceforth, although his name lived on in the Regimental roll of honour, there was always a slight question mark over his reputation.

Whatever had been decided had been worked out between Bowring, the CO of 22 SAS and the Colonel of his own regiment. Surprisingly, not much had been heard of him since, though odd rumours floated around Hereford. After Kelly himself had left, he heard nothing more, despite regular contact with old colleagues and return visits to Stirling Lines.

But whatever Bowring was doing now, Kelly didn't have any doubt that it was serious, and that Bowring took it seriously. It was characteristic of him not to make any concessions in his recruitment of men for his own private operation, whatever it did. So Kelly was prepared to take this test seriously – now, he realized, as much for his own satisfaction as Bowring's.

From his reading of the map, Kelly wasn't too worried about completing the course in time, though he knew he couldn't be complacent. After half an hour of walking up a steady incline, he reached the point where he would have to leave the muddy track, and head up a scree-covered mountainside. He looked up the forty-five-degree slope at the surface of loose shale and the scattered, scrawny bushes. There was little grass to ease the going, and not much to hang on to. He jerked the bergen up his back, tightened the straps and checked his bearing once more before pushing on.

Kelly reached a triangulation point a little after midday. Despite the wet wind, sweat was pouring down his face; his feet and the back of his legs ached viciously. It was time for a halt; fifteen minutes' recuperation should get him back to the same condition he'd been in before he started the main ascent.

Just off the crest of the mountain to the north, there was a large outcrop of shaley rock. He slithered down to it until he was sheltered from the wind in its lea, and hauled off his bergen and unclipped his belt. Using the rucksack as a back rest, he sat down, gulped down a pint of water and ate some dry rations and chocolate.

He gazed out over the naked hilltops and listened to the wind. It was hard to believe he was little more than an hour from the fleshpots of Monaco; it reminded him of the silent hours he had spent in OPs below Mount Kent in East Falkland and on the flanks of the Mourne Mountains of Co. Down.

Suddenly he became alert. That extra sense which

in most of us is only vestigial told him – without being able see, hear or smell anyone – that he was not alone.

A second later, someone was on his back, dragging him sideways to the ground. Even as he keeled over, he had time to reflect ruefully that on an operation he should never have perched in a place like that without checking it out first.

A second man was grabbing his belt from the ground beside him and rifling his open bergen. He'd been jumped by a couple of gypsies.

Kelly rolled like a log out from under his first attacker, and leapt to his feet, poised for the gypsy to come at him. He wished to hell he'd at least been issued with a survival knife. He saw the determination in the hard, high-boned face as the wiry little man launched himself at him.

He looked for the glint of a steel blade, but saw none as he sidestepped the gypsy's attack at the very last moment, grabbed him by his clothing and hurled him headlong down the hillside.

Regaining his breath, he turned his attention to the other man, who scrambled to his feet and sprinted off with all the booty he could carry. Kelly was up with him in half a dozen strides, thrusting his fist into his windpipe. The man was already crumpling when Kelly heard the gunshot behind him. He twisted round, still clutching his captive to use him as a shield.

Piers Bowring, in boots, OGs and a battered Barbour, jumped lightly from the bottom ledge of the crag, holding a 9mm Browning handgun by his side.

'OK, Jack. Quite satisfactory. Now let him go.'

Kelly heaved a sigh of relief.

'For fuck's sake, boss! They never did that to us in the Brecons.'

'No,' Bowring agreed. 'It'd be too risky, but I write my own rules now.' He looked at his watch. 'You'd better get a move on. You've got a detour to make.' Bowring approached as Kelly's victim sank to his knees, gasping. In his hand was a slip of paper. 'Here's the grid ref. And you're still due for target practice at 1700 hours.'

Kelly stifled his questions, gathered up his scattered kit, took another swig of water and heaved the bergen on to his back. He gave Bowring a nod and started off down the hill without a word.

The first gypsy grinned at him as he scrambled back up the slope.

For the rest of the muscle-racking slog, Kelly kept his eyes about him for another attack. It was the first time he'd been on the alert like this since the Gulf. It got his nerves tingling and the adrenalin pumping in a way he had almost forgotten. He felt more alive than he had done at any time in the last three years.

But there were no more attacks. The wind dropped, the clouds broke up. When the sun beamed through by mid-afternoon, he had to take off the Gore-tex and stuff it in his pack. Although his course had been across the grain of the land, over three more peaks as high as the first, he had managed to work up a rhythm which deadened the pain in his calves and ankles. Besides, all his regular running and swimming had kept him at least as fit as he had been when he was fully operational.

And on the stretches of level ground, he was able to think. Whatever Bowring had to offer, if it required this kind of physical condition Kelly wanted it. There was no way he was going to fail this selection.

He guessed that someone must have checked him through the grid refs, but he saw no one besides a lone farmer with his shotgun and a dog, out looking for quail. The farmer had greeted him affably enough in French, without any surprise, probably thinking he was on an exercise up into the mountains from the big French military camp at Canjuer.

Kelly continued up a narrow valley, through a small forest of holm oak and parasol pine, with a mile to go and one last long drag up to the ruins outside Mille Fourches, the last RV. He stopped for a final swig of water and adjusted his straps once more. He had already covered sixteen miles – the detour had added four – one more wouldn't kill him, he thought, almost cheerfully.

The sun was shining obliquely through the tops of the pines, casting occasional beams on the thin scrub of the woodland floor. Birds which had finished foraging for the day were beginning to settle into an afternoon chorus as the remains of the wind lightly rattled the pine needles above and stirred the air, full of the fresh smell of resin and damp earth.

The ground steepened sharply and Kelly found himself alongside a brook, swollen with rain, leaping and glittering down the gully. He scrambled up beside a small waterfall, on to a level clearing twenty yards across. As he started for the further side, his eye was caught by a slight movement in the trees to his left. He stepped back into the bushes and glanced across as two figures emerged from the low scrub.

'It's OK, Jack. You can come out. You've passed your first test.'

It was Terry Haynes. The girl was with him. They both had sporting shotguns broken over their arms and, over his shoulder on a sling, Terry carried an L96 – the new Accuracy International PM sniper rifle, fairly recently added to the standard armoury of 22 SAS.

Kelly grinned back at the cheery weasel face and smiled briefly at the girl, who showed no reaction to his achievement thus far. 'Reminded me of the old days,' he said. 'Does Bowring put all his employees through it?'

'He certainly does. He's not after knackered ex-heroes. Right. Now we've got to see if you can still shoot straight.' Terry hoisted the L96 off his shoulder. 'You've handled one of these?'

'Sure, but I'm more used to the old SSG69.'

'All right. We've got a high seat rigged up on the other side of the clearing, and targets across the valley at eight hundred metres. We'll have a go at those, then we'll wait until the light fades. Michelle needs some practice with the image intensifying and laser sights on closer targets.'

Kelly raised an eyebrow at Michelle. 'You can handle one of those?'

'We'll compare targets later, shall we?' she said.

Kelly dumped the bergen at his feet and said: 'Don't I get an R and R break?'

'Nope. The boss wants to see how you do straight after your walk. The targets are set up.'

'Isn't it a bit risky?'

'Not really. There's a man in the target area making sure there's no one around, and if anyone comes up here, we're after a bit of game. We've got another man at the top of the track too.'

'OK, let's go,' Kelly said, looking forward to proving himself, and warming to the competition provided by the girl. Up in the makeshift highseat, he found he had a clear line of vision across the tops of the pines on the south side of the clearing to a sheer cliff on the other side of the valley, half a mile away.

Through his 12×50 binoculars, Kelly found the targets, two life-sized cut-outs of a French film star, as seen in cinema foyers.

'Which is mine?' he called down to Haynes.

'The one to the east. You've got eight shots and thirty seconds.'

Kelly spread-eagled himself on the timber-plank platform and clicked the bipod down from the front of the stock. He checked that the magazine held eight 7.62mm rounds, then drew back the bolt and slotted one into the breech. With his eye to the telescopic sight, he steadied his breathing and waited for Haynes to start him from his stopwatch.

'Ready. Fire!'

3

Bowring got up from his wicker chair on the terrace. He was wearing a crisp, multicoloured cotton shirt and a fawn linen jacket. He looked as though he had done nothing more strenuous than play bridge all day as he held out a hand to Kelly.

'Congratulations.'

Kelly shook his hand and nodded with a grin.

'No sweat.'

'I wouldn't say that. I can smell you from here. Would you mind changing before we have dinner?' It was not a request. 'We'll talk details then. Terry will take you up to the annexe; there's a room for you there. Dinner will be served here at nine o'clock.'

'Right, boss.'

Kelly walked back into the *salon*.

Haynes was waiting there for him. 'OK? We'll go up in your vehicle.'

Evidently the 'annexe' wasn't adjacent to the villa. Neither man spoke until they were outside the house, walking across to the Range Rover.

'How far is it?' Kelly asked.

'Just up in the village — small house but comfortable.'

'Who else lives there?'

'It depends.'

They climbed into the Range Rover and Kelly started off down the drive.

'I'm usually there, when I'm not on a job,' Haynes went on. 'And anyone else who's over for briefing or training – or sometimes just having a rest. It's not a bad place to be hanging around, here. One thing, though: no pussy on the premises. OK? The boss is very strict about that. As far as the locals are concerned, we're a bunch of guys running a water-skiing school down by the Cap.'

'Anyone else up there now?'

'Yeah. A Jock called Andy Gallagher. Celtic supporter, know what I mean?'

'Ex-military?'

'Yeah. Para. Failed selection for the Regiment; too "self-assertive", they said.'

'Sounds dangerous.'

'He is, but he's got himself under control now. He's done three ops with us, and he's very useful.'

'What sort of ops?'

'I'll leave it up to the boss to tell you all that kind of thing, in case you don't agree to his terms.'

'He wouldn't be letting you take me up to this house if he thought I wasn't going to,' Kelly remarked.

Kelly drove back down to the villa an hour later. He had showered his aching body and clad himself in clean, white cotton trousers and a pale-blue, open-neck shirt. There was no sign now of the morning's wind and rain and the sun had gone down with its customary August orange blaze.

The annexe had turned out to be a stone town house, thoroughly restored and well planned, with four bedrooms and bathrooms. The ground floor was taken up by a large open space which served as kitchen, dining-room and drawing-room. The kitchen showed little sign of regular use, and the whole house had the air of a more than usually sophisticated barrack-room. The small basement had been converted into a fully equipped gymnasium.

Haynes had shown Kelly to a room on the top floor, with a fine view over the roofs of the village to the hills dropping away to the sea. Through the open windows he could hear the sounds of music and laughter drifting up from a small bar two doors down the narrow lane.

The insistent bass thump of soul music seeped beneath the door of the room beside his. When he was on his way down after changing, the door opened.

'Hello.' The delivery was curt, the accent unmistakably Glaswegian.

Kelly nodded a greeting and saw a muscular man, a little younger than himself, in faded shorts, a singlet and flip-flops. Dark hair curled above a tanned, even-featured face from which implausibly innocent blue eyes gazed out at him.

'You the fella who did a selection today?'

'Yeah. Jack Kelly.'

'Andy Gallagher. What did you think of it?'

'I could do with forty-eight hours' serious kip.'

'But you did all right. I checked you through the start and the grid refs. You did a good time. How did you get on with Bowring's ambush?'

Kelly laughed. 'I was lucky. One of them chucked himself down the hillside and smacked his head on a rock. I was just killing the other when the boss showed himself.'

'You were lucky. They're a hard pair those two. And Bowring gives them a bonus if they win. That's why you had no weapons.'

'Sure. I'd worked that out.'

Gallagher had been eyeing Kelly up and down as they spoke. He gave him one last, thoughtful look and said: 'I'll see you, then. We'll have a couple of bevvies.'

The Scot stepped back into his room and closed the door.

Kelly shrugged and carried on down the stairs. As he had assumed, there had been no sign of Michelle at the house. He thought of her as he drove down the hill. And he thought he'd better get any ideas about pursuing her out of his head pretty damn quick. If she was going to be a colleague, there wasn't going to be any room for tricky relationships. And any relationship with a woman who could score as high as she had with the L96 would have to be tricky.

At least, he thought with some satisfaction, he'd scored better than her with the laser sights in the dusk.

He reached the gates and activated them using a remote control which Haynes had given him. As he drove up towards the villa, he took a detailed look at it for the first time.

Below the main floor where the front door and principal rooms were, and beneath the terrace where Bowring had received him earlier, there was another level of rooms, presumably backing on to the cellar where he had been issued with his kit that morning. The front was some sixty feet long, with small cellar windows.

Above were the windows of the *salon*, and possibly another one or two rooms beyond it. The upper two storeys both occupied the same two and a half thousand or so square feet, with half a dozen windows on each front. There was space to accommodate a lot of people and offices. It was, he realized, a much larger building than he'd first thought. And, being where it was, it must have cost a few million. Whatever Bowring was doing, it was clearly making him plenty of money.

Even the gardens, secure behind high walls and other less obvious defences, were beautifully tended and looked like full-time work for at least a couple of men. Kelly was pleased that he was going to be a part of whatever organization funded it all.

He parked the Range Rover on the large gravel forecourt, where a Mercedes 500SL and a brand-new long-wheelbase Land Rover, both French-registered, were already standing.

Strong floodlights, fixed high up the walls of the villa, had been activated as he came up the drive. He was in no doubt that he was already being monitored on a concealed CCTV camera.

The front door opened before he reached the top of the steps. A man, a North African servant of some kind, held the door for him as he passed through.

'Major Bowring waits for you in his office,' the man said in guttural English. He led Kelly up the wide shallow stairs to a room above the *salon* and ushered him in.

Bowring was sitting behind a desk. 'Hello, Jack,' he said. 'Thank you, Omar.'

The servant left, closing the door behind him.

Kelly nodded. 'Major.'

'When we're out and about, we never make reference to any kind of rank or anything that might suggest a military relationship.' It was not a rebuke, but an order. 'Not even "boss".'

'Am I on the team, then?'

'Unless you want to go on providing close personal protection for ungrateful plutocrats.'

Kelly gave a grunt of laughter. 'I think I've had enough of that to be going on with.'

'Good. In which case, sit down and I'll tell you the terms of employment in our organization.' He waved Kelly to a chair opposite him. 'Initially there is a one-year contract, renewable by mutual agreement, which carries a retainer of £50,000, payable in Liechtenstein. For every job in which they participate, team members share ten per cent of the profits. You will be provided with a vehicle, or reimbursed for the use of your own. There will always be accommodation available here, in the village, or at our HQ in England. There are a number of house rules which will be issued to you by our general administrator, Madame Dubrulle.' He looked down at a file open in front of him. 'You aren't married, nor are you conducting any kind of long-term relationship.' He glanced up at Kelly. 'As far as your prospects in this organization are concerned, that's a plus. There are a number of other standing orders, nothing particularly surprising, which you will be required to obey — without exception.' He paused for a few seconds to allow Kelly to absorb the information.

Kelly smiled and nodded.

'Do I take that as your assent to our terms?' Bowring asked.

'I've got a couple of questions,' said Kelly.

Bowring invited them with a raising of his brow. 'What sort of jobs do we do?'

'That's a very broad question. I should tell you right away that we do take on the odd fairly routine sort of work, but only as one-offs, never on long-term contracts – we're far too expensive. Our clients are governments who either do not possess special forces with our particular skills, or who do not wish to involve their own armed forces for one reason or another; and multinational corporations who have to engage from time to time in special projects for which they aren't equipped.' Bowring swivelled his chair round to face the floor-to-ceiling shelves of books behind him. He pressed a button and the whole bookcase slid back and to one side behind its neighbour to reveal a backlit wall map, currently showing Kelly's route march that day. He picked up a control pad and clicked to bring up a geopolitical map of the world.

'In the last year,' he went on, 'we have worked here.' He pointed at a spot in the Amazon basin of Brazil. 'In Uganda, Western Australia, South Korea and here in Bosnia – as well as a lot of one-off escort work.'

Kelly could make intelligent guesses at the nature of the contracts carried out in each location. He nodded appreciatively. 'And what's on the cards now?'

'I'll tell you that once you're signed up.'

'Show me where to sign.'

Bowring allowed himself a quick smile. 'Good man. Here's your contract.' He stood up and walked round the desk, carrying a densely typed three-page document which he handed to Kelly.

The Liverpudlian took it and glanced through it,

picking out the salient points. The contract was between himself and Special Operations Services S.A., registered in Willemstad, Curaçao. 'Got a pen?'

'Don't you want to read it more thoroughly first?'

Kelly shook his head. 'I trust you. Anyway, there wouldn't be a lot of point in your stitching me up, would there?'

Bowring handed him a large black and gold Mont Blanc pen. When Kelly had signed and dated the contract, Bowring picked another from the file on his desk. 'Here's a copy for you, signed by me, so you can have a look at what you've committed yourself to when you have the time.' He held out his hand. 'Welcome to SOS.'

Kelly stood and shook Bowring's hand. 'Thanks,' he grinned.

'Right. We'll go down and join my other dinner guests,' Bowring said, gesturing towards the door.

There were five people already assembled in the *salon*, only one of whom Kelly had seen before.

'I'd like you to meet our newest recruit,' Bowring announced as they walked in. 'Sergeant Jack Kelly, ex-22 SAS, veteran of the Falklands, the Falls Road and Iraq.'

There was a general murmur of approval. Bowring introduced them one by one. 'This is Madame Dubrulle, who looks after money and home comforts, flights and travel arrangements.'

Madame Dubrulle was a short, elegant woman in her mid-fifties. She looked like everyone's favourite aunt and her dark eyes sparkled with perceptive humour.

Bowring then introduced Kelly to a man of a

similar age to Mme Dubrulle, dressed in traditional English summer clothes, much like Bowring. 'Major Lyke, ex-RAOC, who is in charge of supplies and logistics.'

Kelly was introduced to two other men, Michael Dowson, who was described as the London agent, and a Frenchman, Paul Lestienne, Paris agent.

'And Michelle de Lassy, of course, you've already met.'

Michelle smiled. 'Congratulations, Jack.'

The gathering split into two or three groups, and Kelly was left with Michelle.

'Is this the whole firm, then?' he asked.

'No. Besides Terry and Andy up in the village, there are three other permanent soldiers. They're currently on a job in El Salvador. Nothing very exciting. When Major Bowring needs more men, he recruits on a job-by-job basis, but he likes to have about six permanent, selected operatives as a core, so he can always guarantee a certain standard at short notice.'

'Are you a "permanent soldier"?'

'Yes. The major likes to have a good mix of skills. He wanted you for your intelligence-gathering experience and your languages.'

'I've only really got Arabic, and a bit of rough French.'

'And that's always useful. Besides, we needed a replacement.'

Kelly wondered if this was as a result of a resignation, dismissal or death. Before he could ask, they were joined by Major Lyke.

'Welcome aboard, Jack.'

'Thanks, Major.'

'Call me Bob. You're not in the British Army now.'

'I can tell that by the lifestyle,' Kelly laughed, as a maid who had come in and circulated among the guests handed him a glass of champagne.

'There are downsides to that as well, though,' Lyke remarked, without wistfulness. 'Risking your life, not for Queen and Country, just for the money. Still, there it is. It's a dirty job, but someone's got to do it.'

'And what is the next job?' Kelly asked.

'That's what we're all here for. Piers Bowring doesn't give dinner parties out of any sense of social duty. So I suggest you don't drink too much. The briefing comes after.'

Dinner was served in a large, classically French dining-room which, like the *salon*, looked out towards the sea.

Kelly was placed between Mme Dubrulle and Michael Dowson. The conversation was generally not 'shop', as if it were tacitly accepted there would be more of that later.

Madame Dubrulle, who asked Kelly to call her Colette, wanted to know all about him: his childhood, his marriage, life in Herefordshire, his recent job looking after little Béatrice Skiapoulos, who was regularly featured as a poor little rich girl in the French gossip magazines.

Dowson was less talkative. Kelly discovered very little about him or his background. In his late thirties, on the face of it he was a typical ex-public school stockbroker type, except that he seemed exceptionally well informed on current world affairs. But he was friendly enough and treated Kelly as a colleague and equal. It appeared that he was well acquainted with his service record and was prepared to grant him the credit he deserved.

After dinner, towards midnight, the party moved upstairs to Bowring's office on the first floor. There were enough seats to accommodate them all, while Bowring stood behind his desk and clicked the map back into view. In his hand he held, from habit, his old cavalry whip as a pointer.

'Right, ladies and gentlemen, Operation Parson's Nose.'

Kelly smiled, but the others showed no sign of mirth. Evidently it was Bowring's wont to give his contracts silly names.

'Our client is the Vatican State. We are instructed by the second in command to Archbishop O'Keane, who is responsible for security. As you may know, the Vatican has one of the best intelligence services in the world – a result, no doubt, of skills learned in the confessional. With a few hundred million pairs of ears listening on their behalf, there isn't much they don't get to hear about sooner or later. Through their legation in Damascus, they have received the information that a group calling itself Sufuf Allah is preparing an attack on the Pope some time within the next four weeks.'

Bowring pointed at his map. 'His Holiness's itinerary takes him to India for three days at the end of this month, and then he starts his six-day tour of the UK, or, I should say, England, Scotland and Wales; kissing the ground of Ulster was considered too risky. Though they have as yet no information to confirm it, the Vatican officials feel that the attack will be made on one of these two tours.'

'Why not at the Vatican itself?' Bob Lyke asked.

'Security there is surprisingly sophisticated, particularly after the last assassination attempt. Don't forget, they have a force of four hundred Swiss Guards to draw on. In any event, phase one of our job is to try to make direct contact with their informant, establish if he is in it out of idealism, or for the money, and see if he can put us anywhere nearer Sufuf Allah.'

'What do we know about these Sufuf Allah?' Paul Lestienne asked.

'Not a lot. I'd never heard of them before. I suspect it's a very small organization, and probably too militant for most of the mainstream groups to have much truck with. If they are seriously planning the Pope's assassination, it will be an opening propaganda gambit, to establish their credentials and pull in more like-minded recruits.'

'Where are they based?'

'We assume in Lebanon, but it could just as well be Iraq or Jordan. Anyway, they could be drawing from Islamic extremist groups from several countries.'

'Do we assume,' Lestienne asked, 'that this imminent attack has some bearing on the Vatican exchanging ambassadors with Israel?'

'Of course.'

'Then is it not likely that there would be a strong Palestinian element to any group wishing to show their objection?'

'Not necessarily. The destruction of the State of Israel is a tenet vigorously held by a diverse number of Islamic groups. Naturally, there may be a Palestinian factor.'

He paused, aware of the scantiness of information. 'Once we've established where they're coming from, our brief is straightforward enough: to destroy the task force, as close to the projected attempt as possible, so they don't have time to regroup and send in others and so not waste whatever logistical arrangements they've made.'

Bowring put down his whip and leaned forward with both his hands flat on the table. He looked at each of them in turn.

Christ, Kelly thought, it's a terrible brief, and he knows it. Three weeks to track down and take out an unknown number of Muslim loonies planning to kill a man who would be publicly exposed to hundreds of thousands of people at a time.

No one spoke for several seconds, then Lyke asked: 'What's the money like?'

One side of Bowring's mouth twitched. 'That's the good bit. Top rate daily fee and all exes, and a million-dollar performance bonus.'

'I'm not surprised,' Lyke murmured.

Bowring turned to Dowson. 'You brought this job in, Michael. Is there anything you can add to what I've said?'

Dowson leant back in his chair. 'When I first met our contact in Rome, he did surmise that the original lead might have come from a source in Amman.' Dowson shrugged his neatly clad shoulders. 'But if he didn't tell you, I guess it was fairly conjectural.'

'He did. That will be our starting-point.' He glanced at Kelly. 'Jack and I will be leaving for Jordan, via Rome, tomorrow evening, Colette.'

Madame Dubrulle nodded and made a note on a pad on her knees.

Kelly felt a flush of elation that he was going into action so soon.

'Bob, you and Michael can go over all the details of the Pope's two tours and identify likely sites for a hit,' Bowring continued. 'In case it's planned for the UK, we'll have to top up the armoury at Summerfold – two full complements of weapons and ammunition for four men. Use the boat into a small east coast marina.'

Major Lyke nodded. 'Who will you want on the job?'

'Jack here, Andy, Terry for communications, and Michelle. If we have to, we can pull Mick Young back from San Salvador. It depends on the size of unit we're up against.'

'And will you be active?'

Bowring nodded. 'I will be on this one. It could get complicated.'

Kelly woke from a deep sleep to a standard Côte d'Azur summer morning.

Haynes was brewing coffee when he went down-stairs. There was a bag of fresh croissants on the table. 'Morning, mate. Feeling better?' said the Londoner.

'Fucking stiff. I'm going for a run to loosen up.'

'You're expected up at the villa in just over an hour, so make it quick. I'll leave a few of these for you if you like.' Haynes nodded at the bag on the table.

'Thanks.'

Kelly set off at a comfortable lope through the lanes of the village and down the switchback road towards the coast. Half an hour and seven miles later, he was back in the kitchen with a bowl of coffee in front of him.

At the villa, he was shown down some back stairs, not behind the hall panelling this time, leading to the rooms below. There he found Madame Dubrulle and Bob Lyke, each in an office reflecting their own personal tastes; hers full of flowers, his lined with regimental photographs and paintings of recent engagements by units of the British Army.

Colette Dubrulle showed him round a further office housing two secretaries and an advanced communications room. 'This is Terry's domain, though Bob can operate most of it,' she said.

There was an air of quiet efficiency about the place. From the charts and maps on the walls, it was obvious that there was a lot more going on than Bowring had revealed.

'How come there are so many of you involved in administration here?' Kelly asked, wondering if he'd get an honest answer.

Colette gave him a smile. 'Major Bowring didn't have time last night to tell you much about the background to our organization. He asked me to explain. Come into my office. I'll get some coffee.'

They went back to the bright, Provençal furnishings of her room, where she sat Kelly in a wicker armchair.

'This villa and these offices belong to Achilles International Couriers S.A. We operate one of the largest courier services in this part of the Mediterranean. It is a successful and very profitable business in its own right. It is also a very effective cover for the operation of SOS. As far as the French authorities are concerned, Major Bowring has no connection with it. Bob Lyke and Ferdinand Gatti, who is a lawyer from Monaco, are the directors. We also own a small boat-hire and water-skiing company called Hydra-Jet, down at Beausoleil. As far as the locals are concerned, that's who you work for. You should put in an appearance there now and again, and if no one's using the boats, you can.'

'Quite a set-up, then,' Kelly said.

'There are a few other activities as well, but not important for you. Of course, the existence of SOS must be kept secret. If you've read your contract, you'll have seen that.'

Colette also gave Kelly a letter of agreement between himself and the boat-hire company, purporting to make use of his services as an instructor; a folder containing information about Achilles Couriers; and a set of house rules. 'Make sure you read them,' she said. 'Major Bowring won't take any deviation from them. It's all in your contract.'

Kelly felt inclined to resent this degree of regulation, but on the other hand, he was used to it from his army days, and it was a small price to pay for the chance of some real action again.

'Now,' the Frenchwoman went on. 'We need a set of photographs for IDs and passports and we must get a letter to your previous employers tendering your resignation. I have a certificate here that says your ankle is badly damaged and you will be unable to undertake any physical duties for at least six weeks. You shouldn't have a problem, but let me have your old contract and I will sort it out.'

Kelly didn't see Bowring again until that evening on the flight from Nice to Rome. They sat at opposite ends of the plane and didn't communicate or acknowledge each other. It was only when they had booked into separate hotels in Rome and Kelly was in his room that he got a call from Bowring.

'I'll be over in twenty minutes. Take a walk round the block to make sure you haven't been followed.'

Kelly was accustomed, from his years in the SAS, to the notion of maximum intelligence gathering – leaving as little as possible to even the slimmest chance. That anyone might have shadowed him from the town house in Roquebrune to the airport, and then arranged to have him trailed from Leonardo da Vinci to his hotel in Rome was very unlikely indeed. But it was possible, and it he could be absolutely certain one way or the other by going out to see if he picked up a tail.

Through the narrow streets behind the Corso Vittorio Emanuele II, he set off at a fast walk on a circuitous journey, but always heading in approximately the same direction to give plausibility to his route. He entered a quiet residential street with one or two shops and walked a hundred yards until he reached an antique shop. He glanced in the window, apparently spotted something that took his eye and went in.

Inside, waving away the attentions of the proprietor, he held up an unframed print of the Colosseum as if to study it. But he kept his eyes fixed on the window, through which he had a clear view of the street, checking every man and woman that passed on either side of the road. He took a mental photograph of each of them, identifying a particular characteristic in each that would help his memory.

After a minute, Kelly apologized with a polite shrug for the fact that the print wasn't quite what he wanted, thanked the proprietor and left. He repeated the process in a picture gallery three streets and four turns further on.

He recognized none of the passers-by from his first stop, but went through the same mental photography. He had reached a large, open *piazza* now. He gave himself an excuse to run by stepping in front of a tide of unforgiving traffic as the lights turned green.

Kelly sprinted, as if for his life, across the square and into a small street on the other side. Near the corner, he bumped into an old woman coming in the other direction, which gave him the chance to take a quick glance over his shoulder. No one else had followed his suicidal dash. He carried on, hoping that he would be able to double back on himself, and before long he found a small alley, opening to the left. Relieved to see that it was open-ended, he ducked into it. He walked very quickly to the far end, turned left again, and arrived back on the corner of the square he'd just crossed. He saw no one he recognized from his two stops at the galleries.

He went into a bar, ordered and downed a small espresso, then set off back towards the hotel, satisfied that no one was following him.

Bowring arrived soon afterwards with a woman.

'The Contessa di Francisci looks after our interests in Italy,' Bowring said without preamble. 'Anna-Teresa, this is Jack Kelly.'

Kelly shook hands with the woman.

'It's a pleasure to meet you,' she said with a slight American accent. She looked, Kelly thought, more like the editor of a fashion magazine than an agent for a bunch of mercenaries.

She turned to Bowring. 'Monsignor di Montefalco will see you tomorrow morning. I have also had lunch today with a friend of mine in the Vatican press office. He was surprisingly indiscreet.'

'I'm sure it came as no surprise to you,' Bowring said.

She smiled. 'I was able to learn a little about the monsignor's boss, Archbishop O'Keane, as you asked. The Archbishop comes from Chicago, where the Church is having a hard time from women's groups over female ordination. He feels that His Holiness takes too firm a line on the question. Besides they already have big problems there trying to sell the official line on contraception.'

Bowring was looking at her thoughtfully. 'You feel this has some relevance?'

The Contessa lifted a narrow shoulder. 'It could have.'

'What about our friend Montefalco?'

'He has a reputation for being very orthodox.'

'You don't surprise me. What's his background?'

'Rather a grand family, though impoverished. He was an outstanding student at the University of Florence; he read theology and history. There is no scandal about him, but he is not well liked.'

'Not really one of the boys, eh?' Bowring gave a short laugh. 'He found it hard to approve of me, yet, realistically, he knew he had to. I don't know much about the inner workings of the Catholic Church, but I suppose, like any successful organization, pragmatism gets the better of ideology. You're a Catholic, aren't you, Jack? What do you think?'

'I'm afraid pragmatism came out on top a long time ago,' Kelly said quickly. 'I've seen what lack of birth control can do to a family. But I'm not too up-to-date on it all now.'

'Really,' the Contessa said, 'for practical purposes, you're dealing with a political body here, rather than a religious organization.'

Bowring nodded. 'That's the impression I have already. What is important to us – I mean to our own personal safety – is just how discreet these people are.'

'Very. Knowledge of SOS or yourself will be restricted almost certainly to the few people who are closest to it now. I'm certain that Monsignor di Montefalco was telling you the truth when he said that His Holiness doesn't know about this plot, and they'll want to keep it that way. As few people as possible will be told, if any more than know already. It's possible, I suppose, that something might leak back from the legation in Damascus.' She shrugged. 'I don't know anything about Rappacioli, the nuncio there, but I doubt it. A man in that posting would be a diplomat above all else.'

Bowring was silent for a moment.

'OK, Anna-Teresa. Thanks. Keep your ears open and report back to Bob Lyke, We'll be leaving for Amman as soon as we've seen Montefalco tomorrow. Now, I propose dinner somewhere civilized but discreet.'

Kelly walked back from the small restaurant in the Via Sicilia. The Contessa was dropping Bowring back at his hotel in her car. Kelly wondered if it was more than a purely professional liaison, but decided it wasn't. Certainly, Bowring seemed very relaxed, almost intimate in his dealings with her, but then, such was his own self-assurance, he could adopt such an attitude at will if he thought it would serve his purpose.

Kelly had seen him do it, with senior police officers in Northern Ireland and his superiors in the
Falklands. Bowring, he knew, was well versed in the
petty political skirmishes that surrounded battlefield
decision-making.

But Kelly was not prepared for his boss's appearance when he arrived at his hotel next morning.
He didn't even recognize the bearded cleric until
he spoke.

'I'm Father Babbington now,' Bowring announced,
without a hint of humour, 'until further notice and as
long as I'm in this outfit. I've seen Montefalco. He's
organized all the documentation I need. Anna-Teresa
will be round shortly with your ticket, ID and hotel
details in Amman. You are there as a representative of a small British firm dealing in second-hand
agricultural vehicles. Register with the Embassy as
soon as you arrive and I'll have made various other
arrangements for you. In principle, if possible you
and I shouldn't make direct contact in Jordan. But
I'll get instructions to you tonight. Best of luck, and
keep your head down.'

4

The heat blasted off the runways of Amman's international airport, making them shimmer. Kelly stepped out of an ALIA aircraft and sniffed the dry wind blowing off the great Saudi desert and his nose twitched at the familiar smells. Bowring was already easing himself fastidiously on to an airport bus.

As well as documents identifying him as Father Henry Babbington, an English Catholic priest and a temporarily accredited member of the Vatican diplomatic service, Bowring was carrying in his shoulder bag two Browning 9mm handguns and fifty parabellum rounds which he had arranged to pass on to Kelly at the Intercontinental Hotel that evening.

He received a few stares but passed without trouble through the terminal building. The sight of a European in a clerical collar was not common in the streets or indeed the diplomatic receptions of Jordan, where barely five per cent of the population were Christian. But Bowring intended to be noticed, and expected questions to be asked.

He had arranged to stay at the residence of the British Defence Attaché, rather than the Papal legation. It hadn't been hard to organize; he had been in the same regiment as the man currently occupying the post. 'Why, may I ask, are you posing as a Catholic priest?' Bowring's host enquired. They were walking together in the privacy of the lush gardens of the Ambassador's residence before the small monthly reception for visiting British businessmen which was taking place that evening.

Bowring was unconvinced by Colonel Giles Wilkinson's display of bluff bone-headedness. At the same time, he was aware that he was seriously compromising his friend. He guessed Wilkinson had agreed to have him purely out of curiosity, and the possibility that there might be an intelligence quid pro quo.

'I'm following up some information for my clients.'

'I'm not sure that I should be harbouring a freelance spy, particularly one disguised like you.'

'Why not? I dare say you have plenty of so-called "friends" from MI6 in the embassy.'

'Look, Piers, unless you can tell me something about your current contract, I can't be much help. And if you want your cover left intact, you'll have to make sure you keep out of trouble.'

'Frankly, Giles, there's not a lot to tell. I'm gambling on the probability that the presence of a visiting Vatican diplomat in town will flush out an informant. It's a long shot, but of course, if I get anything of value to HMG, I'll pass it on.'

'Of course,' Colonel Wilkinson said drily. He, and his superiors, though in principle disapproving of all freelances, had too much respect for Bowring's reputation to dissuade or impede him — at least, until he had had a chance to discover something worthwhile. The Vatican wouldn't have called him in without a strong lead and, by the same token, a potentially dangerous one.

In a way that was almost uniquely British, the two men, by tacit agreement, dropped the topic and began to swap information about mutual friends.

As they talked, Bowring considered his own plans.

It made sense to him that the information which had reached the ears of Rappacioli, the nuncio in Damascus, should have filtered up from Amman. Despite the British-educated monarch's aversion to the more outspoken representatives of Islam, and his generally benign approach to the West, angry Muslims were relatively safe going about their business in the Jordanian capital, where Palestinian refugee camps had created an unmonitorable population of itinerants.

It was also logical that information of interest to the Christian community should have been passed up the line into Syria, with its substantially larger Christian population, there to reach one of the most important Papal legations in the Middle East.

Whether the informant's motive had been financial or ideological, there was a more than reasonable chance that the presence of a visiting Vatican diplomat would flush him, or her, out.

Kelly pushed one of the Brownings into his shoulder holster and pulled on a loose linen jacket. He had picked up the package containing the handguns and ammunition from the lavatories of the main lobby of the Intercontinental, from the cubicle just vacated by the sober-looking, bearded priest. Before that he had spent an hour reading what scanty information he had been supplied with on the state of the Jordanian market for tractors and combines, enough at least to get him out of trouble if he found himself in a corner.

In the two days he had worked for Bowring's organization, Kelly had been impressed by the efficiency and thoroughness with which such things as alternative identities and travel arrangements had been made. A complete set of documents and passport had simply been handed to him with his ticket an hour before he set off for Nice airport.

He had hired a car as instructed. His brief was to attend the reception that evening at the Ambassador's residence to establish his temporary credentials.

The following morning, he was to be ready at eight to tail Bowring from the Defence Attaché's house to wherever he might happen to go. He was only to make his presence felt in circumstances of extreme danger, either to Bowring or to any informant who might appear. Otherwise, his was a watching brief.

A hundred yards from the gates of the Defence Attaché's residence, Kelly waited in his hired Toyota, with the blinds down, the Browning in his holster, and a pair of binoculars and a Pentax with a compact 600mm telephoto lens on the seat beside him. He had to wait over an hour before he saw Bowring climb into a taxi and head for the centre of town.

Amman, built on rolling hills to the east of the Ajlun Mountains, had largely, and hurriedly, been constructed since the country had gained independence from the British Mandate in 1949. A thousand dusty alleys gave off wide, European-style two-lane thoroughfares. Bridges crossed the dry, litter-filled courses of the Wadi Amman and its tributaries. The city's population of a million or so was largely influenced by sporadic influxes of Palestinian Arabs, particularly after the Arab-Israeli War of 1967 and their expulsion from Lebanon. But the Palestinians, like their Israeli cousins, are an industrious tribe, and despite its natural shortcomings as a centre for industry and trade, and the lack of resources of the nation as a whole, Amman bustled with commercial activity, especially since the destruction of Beirut.

Kelly had to dodge buses, trucks, ramshackle cars, donkeys pulling carts and unwary, black-clad women to keep up with Bowring's taxi. But he stuck with it and after fifteen minutes it pulled up outside the Hotel Philadelphia, an uninspired sixties construction on the edge of the old quarter.

Bowring climbed out of the taxi and walked into the hotel. The driver stayed where he was, evidently instructed to wait. Kelly found a gap to park his car from where he could see the entrance to the hotel, pulled down all but one of the blinds and waited.

Systematically, he checked every man, woman and child he could see within the vicinity of the hotel. He made a note of the trickle of people entering and leaving it. Relying on his own judgement, he photographed all those he thought might have dealings with Bowring, or be interested in those dealings.

Bowring walked into the hotel's gloomy, lacklustre café, sat on a bentwood chair at a small table and ordered a coffee from a sleepy waiter.

Having cast his bait in the water so recently, he was almost suspicious that he had had a bite so soon. But the taxi had turned up without warning at the Defence Attaché's house, its driver announcing that he had come to take Father Babbington to his meeting. News of his presence could have been relayed by any of the Ambassador's Arab staff, who would have noted his presence at the reception the evening before. The success of this stage of the operation and, for that matter, his own personal safety, depended on which side had received the news.

Although he'd known that Kelly wouldn't be far behind him, he himself was unarmed. That he had been deposited at this seedy hotel gave Bowring considerable relief; it was unlikely that anyone had brought him here to kill him.

The waiter returned without his coffee.

'Come,' he said, beckoning Bowring to follow him.

With some misgivings, Bowring let himself be led from the room, across a small hallway and up a narrow flight of service stairs. They passed along a dingy first-floor corridor until they reached a door guarded by two young, slouching Palestinians who each placed a hand inside their denim jean jackets with a deliberateness that conveyed an obvious message. Bowring showed no reaction to them as the waiter opened a door to a small, plain bedroom at the back of the building. He walked in.

Sitting on the bed was a large, prosperous-looking Arab in a well-pressed linen suit. He was stout, respectable, with an air of benign cosmopolitanism. Bowring judged he was a businessman, rather than a politician, of about fifty.

The man climbed laboriously to his feet.

'Father Babbington?'

Bowring nodded.

'*Salaam a leykum.*'

'*A leykum, salaam.*' Bowring returned his small bow.

'I am Said Shalawi. I understand that you are on a mission from the Vatican State?' He spoke good

English but in the manner of someone who has learnt the language from out-of-date textbooks.

'That's correct.'

'I had been expecting someone to come. I was responsible for certain information reaching Damascus. Do you know what I am talking about?'

Bowring nodded. 'We are engaged in the same matter.'

'Good. As I thought. I can tell you nothing here, you understand. It was risky even for me to come here, but it is my cousin's place, so I can enter unseen. You may have been watched, but that was a necessary risk. I have certain documents which I can give to you elsewhere.'

'Where are they now?'

'In my office in Beirut. If you will meet me in Paris next week, I will take them there and show you them. It is also possible that I may have more information by then.'

'Are you selling this information?'

'I will tell you why I want you to hear it. It is in the best interests of the whole business community, here and in Lebanon, that there should be peace between Arabs and Israelis. If the problems with the West Bank settlers can be resolved, and the people of Palestine allowed to resume their lives in the place of their birth, it will bring untold benefits to the prosperity of the whole region. I myself have done a considerable amount of business with Tel Aviv,' he added with some smugness. 'However, an international incident of the type which is being planned will harden the resolve of the entrenched right-wing Israelis and convince the waiverers that the Arab world is still committed to their destruction. My greatest wish is to see the current peace process brought to a happy conclusion.'

Bowring searched the man's earnest eyes for signs of altruism. He came to the conclusion that he was dealing with a man whose commercial interests happened to coincide with the aims of the peacemakers. It was a sound, reliable enough motive.

'Good,' said Bowring. 'I am instructed by my superiors that we will naturally meet any expenses you may incur in relaying this information to us.'

Shalawi nodded. He wasn't averse to any bonuses that might be on offer. 'That is generous. One of my associates has a house near Paris. I will be there next week. I will be able to give you the information then. I cannot here – there are too many eyes watching, too many people ready to torture and to kill to guard their secrets. I will leave details of place and date for you at the Hôtel Griffon in St Germain. Do not go yourself. Send a messenger, who must ask for a letter to M. Lorin about the Nicosia Project. Now you must go. *Inshallah*, your visit to this place has not been noted.'

Bowring and Shalawi bowed to each other again and Bowring let himself out of the room and went downstairs to the waiting taxi.

Kelly flicked up the blinds, dropped his camera on the passenger seat and started the car. He had photographed a dozen or so possible watchers. But he had seen no one go into the hotel after Bowring who looked like a candidate for their informant.

He pulled out behind the taxi and followed it, several cars back, until it drew up outside the Intercontinental. He pulled in and waited while Bowring got out and walked briskly inside. He was about to follow when he spotted a man get out of a Subaru pick-up which had arrived behind Bowring's taxi.

His guts tightened with an adrenalin rush; it was one of the men he had photographed outside the Hotel Philadelphia. Slim, dark-skinned, denim-clad, the man was maybe in his twenties. He walked confidently into the hotel lobby.

Unhurriedly, Kelly slung his camera over his shoulder, got out of his car and sauntered into the hotel. The young Arab was talking earnestly to one of the uniformed hotel porters. Kelly allowed his leisurely passage towards the cigarette kiosk to take him close to them. Without obviously dawdling, he heard the porter insisting that he hadn't seen the English priest before. The other, in a harsher Palestinian accent, pressed him. Kelly was unable to hear any reply. But it seemed that the porter, not surprisingly, was entirely ignorant about Bowring's, or Father Babbington's, identity.

As he bought a packet of cigarettes, Kelly's eyes swept the lobby for a sign of Bowring. There was none. He bought the *Daily Telegraph* and walked across to lower himself into one of a group of club chairs scattered about the marble floor of the huge foyer. He opened his paper and lifted it no higher than would allow his eyes to continue scanning the hall.

He watched the slim, blue figure of Bowring's pursuer walk swiftly over to the hall porters' desk, where he was met with an angry shaking of heads. The man dithered for a moment then, making up his mind, headed for the main doors once again. Kelly waited until he was through them before he stirred himself.

A minute later he was quietly easing the Toyota out on to the road with four cars between him and his quarry's Subaru pick-up. He guessed the Palestinian had thought that a Vatican envoy in town might spell trouble, though any connection with their own plans was only a remote possibility. It was certainly possible, Kelly reckoned, that this group, these Sufuf Allah, had a source of general information within the British Embassy.

It seemed unlikely that a two-handed team had been on to Bowring, or that he himself had been identified as having any connection with Father Babbington. But he kept a close look in his mirror until he was convinced that he had no tail on him. The Subaru had by this time recrossed the seething centre of Amman and was on the main road south towards Jerusalem.

After a few miles they were approaching a sprawling refugee shanty town when, as Kelly had feared, the pick-up turned off and dived down among the makeshift streets. As a European, he couldn't follow there without arousing suspicion, for it was scarcely a recognized tourist destination.

He drove on for a mile or so, turned and drove back past the refugee camp. With a sense of anticlimax and disappointment, he allowed some of the tension to drain from his system. It came as a slight shock to him to discover just how turned on he had been by the thought that he might, after a long lay-off, have had a chance to deploy a weapon in anger.

In fact, what he had achieved was a lot more useful than disposing of Bowring's tail; he had a photo in the can of someone very likely connected with, if not actually a member of, Sufuf Allah.

He drove back to the Intercontinental with the

aim of getting in contact with Bowring through the Embassy. But Bowring had pre-empted him. There was a curt note waiting for him: 'Your return flight booked for tomorrow. Collect details from commercial section at embassy.'

Bowring, beardless and looking his usual elegant self in a creaseless lightweight suit, was waiting for Kelly at Charles de Gaulle. He had a hired Citroën in the car park. Ten minutes after clearing customs, Kelly was sitting beside his boss on the autoroute back into Paris.

'When did you stop being Father Babbington?' he asked.

'When I arrived here last night.'

'Why did you leave so fast?'

'I'd got all I was going to get in Amman, and I dare say you noticed I was followed back to your hotel.'

'I did. I'd already got a shot of him. When he lost you in the hotel, I followed him back to a refugee camp on the Jerusalem road. But there was no way I could go in there.'

'Quite right. That's very good news, that you got a photo.'

'What did you get in the Hotel Philadelphia?'

'My clerical persona worked like a mayfly on a hungry trout,' Bowring said with a trace of self-satisfaction. 'I was taken there on the instructions of a man, a Palestinian of pragmatic outlook by the name of Said Shalawi.'

'What's his brief, then?' Kelly asked.

'Frankly, I'm not sure of his motives. It's probably fair to say that he's a natural dove, but I suspect he's just beginning to get deals together between Beirut and Tel Aviv and he doesn't want to see them blown out of the water before they're launched.'

'What did he tell you?'

'Nothing,' Bowring said. 'But he'll be here next week, with some kind of documentary back-up to his information.'

'Does he want paying for it?'

'Yes, though, as I say, I think that is a secondary motive. Of course, it's possible he represents broader interests in Beirut. After all, now that the place is being rebuilt again and business is starting to flow back, no one wants to risk a return to the mayhem of the eighties. He was prepared to tell me very little, and I suspect he gave me a false name; he felt there was some possibility that if it were known I'd been in contact with him, someone might try to extract anything he'd given me.' Bowring cleared his throat. 'That's why I saw no point in hanging around.'

'Do you think you were checked out of the airport?'

'Impossible to say. I doubt it, though, and anyway, if they start looking, they'll find that Father Babbington has disappeared up his own cassock.'

Kelly laughed. 'And they'll never make the connection between him and you. I didn't know you had the talent.'

'It's one I've developed since my days in the Regiment. I once tested it at a family funeral. There were a couple of dozen people who knew me there, but not one recognized me. It's been rather useful from time to time, in an intelligence-gathering capacity.'

'Anyway,' Kelly said. 'What's the form now?'

'Instructions will be left for us at a place called the Hôtel Griffon. Shalawi is coming to Paris next week, but he didn't say when precisely. In the meantime, I want you to check it out, for any comings and goings. We mustn't overlook the fact that Shalawi could be a red herring.'

'You'd better turn back into Father Babbington, when you see him, just in case.'

'Naturally. In the meantime, we're both staying at Paul Lestienne's in suburban splendour in Maisons-Laffitte. As a matter of fact, as I recall you have a taste for that sort of thing, I can tell you there's a small race meeting there this evening. First race is at five-thirty. You could just make it if I start driving like a native.'

Since he had been working in France, Kelly had made a habit of following the form of French horses. He had been a regular visitor to the *hippodrome* in Cagnes-sur-Mer. It had given him the slightest touch of homesickness to see some of the British-trained horses and their entourages trying to score some prize money and early-season experience in February.

He went to the races that evening and made the most of it for an hour or two, though he had the feeling Bowring was giving him the chance to relax a bit before the real action started. He came away with a good profit and arrived back at Lestienne's small mansion in the woods feeling ready for anything.

Lestienne introduced his wife and suggested that they go out for dinner. Bowring would join them later. Anxious to find out more about Special Operations Services S.A., Kelly agreed. However, it was soon clear that either Lestienne didn't discuss his business in public places, or his wife had no idea what sort of business he was in. He asked Kelly a little about his experiences in the Falklands, discussed the political situation in Northern Ireland with a surprising amount of knowledge and insight, and led the discussion on to international politics in general.

When Bowring joined them, much later than expected and making no excuses for it, the conversation still remained firmly aloof from the job in hand. But later, over large glasses of cognac and calvados, as the three men sat comfortably in Lestienne's spacious drawing-room, the matter of Shalawi was finally raised.

'When we have an address,' Bowring said to Lestienne, 'we'll need to have the place thoroughly staked out, even though we won't have a lot of time to organize it. Get Andy and Terry up from Roquebrune tomorrow, and find me three or four locals. You should be able to get some from Paul's Bar, but no dross, please, and for God's sake don't tell them SOS are involved.'

Lestienne nodded. Paul's Bar was an earthy drinking dive off the Place de la République, where ex- and jobless mercenaries and legionnaires gathered, to keep their ears open for any work that was going. 'There's a trio of ex-South African Recon Commandos just arrived. They came to see me last week. They looked useful but they have a pretty grand idea of their own value.'

'I'll have a look at them,' Bowring said. 'Fix it up.'

On the Monday of the following week, Kelly took a morning commuter train into Gare St Lazare. At that time of year, the train, like the whole of Paris, was half empty. Kelly, in open-neck shirt, light tweed jacket and thin beige cords looked comfortable, like a graphic artist or journalist just back from his holidays.

Once in Paris, he took the Métro to Rue du Bac, emerged into the Boulevard Raspail, and walked into the nearest *café-tabac*. He bought *Le Figaro* and a packet of Gitanes, sat down and ordered an espresso. He pulled a small map of Paris from his pocket and checked the location of the Hôtel Griffon. It was less than two hundred yards from where he was sitting, but in the next street off the main thoroughfare, not visible from the café. He finished his coffee, folded his paper under his arm and sauntered out into the street. A few minutes later he was walking with a purposeful stride along a narrow, car-lined street of private apartment houses, small antique shops and a bakery.

Fifty yards from the junction with Boulevard Raspail, he passed the Hôtel Griffon. It was one of those small Parisian hotels which the proprietors have never found it necessary to update, since they are cheap enough to generate no great expectations of luxury from their clientele. Kelly judged it might contain twenty or thirty rooms. He looked around for a suitable OP. There was no bar in the street but almost opposite the hotel was an antiquarian bookshop. That would have to do for an initial recce. After Kelly had browsed and leafed through twenty books over an hour or so, the bookseller was becoming restive. But during that time, Kelly had been able to gain some idea from the comings and goings of the clientele of the Hôtel Griffon.

In addition to various Europeans – businessmen,

tourists and students – a large proportion of the people he had seen entering and leaving the hotel were Arabs, Middle Eastern rather than North African, for the most part reasonably prosperous and conservatively dressed in western business suits. There were many reasons for Syrians and Lebanese to be visiting Paris, commercially and culturally, so there was nothing odd about a particular hotel having built up a connection, with regular visitors from those countries. In any case, it was possible that the place was owned and managed by Arabs. On the face of it, it was a perfectly plausible place for this contact of Bowring's to leave his instructions.

Aware that he had used up his browsing time, Kelly gratified the bookseller by buying an 1840 edition of Balzac's *Le Père Goriot*, and walked out of the shop clutching it with the smugness of a contented collector. He had at least created a precedent for a few more long visits there.

Later, Kelly met his boss among the anonymous, bustling tourists in the Deux Magots. They sat at the back of the cavernous café and ordered beers.

'What have we got?' Bowring asked.

'Looks OK. Lot of Arabs. Not Gulf – not rich enough – but businessmen, mostly. Didn't see anyone that worried me, but I only watched for an hour or so; had to buy this book. Can I get it back on exes?' He dropped the leatherbound book on the table in front of Bowring, who picked it up and flicked through it with interest.

'Sure. It's a good edition,' Bowring said, closing the book carefully. 'How do you want to go about it now?'

'I'll need a car for an OP. Fifty yards or so from the entrance, out of sight of any of the bedroom windows. That's the only real chance of keeping a long watch without moving into a building opposite.'

'We haven't got time for that. OK, get a car ... no, a van. You'll just have to sit there until Andy and Terry arrive tonight, then you'll have to roster with them.'

Bowring saw the look of resignation on Kelly's face. 'There won't be too much of this. I'm paying you too much to waste you on passive surveillance. And, who knows, you might get a target out of it.'

'You think so?'

'No. I think Shalawi's genuine. But you know how it is.'

Kelly knew how it was. The survival of a unit depended on reducing risks to the minimum, and eliminating intelligence deficiencies. It was bloody boring, but the more you knew about your enemy when you went in, the more confidently and efficiently you fought them.

By Wednesday, after sharing eight-hour turns with Gallagher and Haynes, they had seen no one who aroused their professional suspicions, or matched Kelly's shot of the young Palestinian who had tailed Bowring in Amman.

Bowring reverted to the persona of Father Henry Babbington and dispatched one of the South Africans to the hotel to ask, as instructed, for the letter to M. Lorin about the Nicosia Project. The burly ex-soldier returned to the rendezvous at the Solférino Métro station with an envelope. Bowring opened it and read the few words on the single piece of paper inside.

'He's not taking chances. I'll be met in front of the Hôtel des Invalides one hour from when you collected this letter. Tell Andy I want you all there, singly, staked out, and Terry in the van in case I get taken.'

Terry Haynes sat in the anonymous Renault van which Kelly had hired to watch the Hôtel Griffon. He was parked illegally, ready to drive round the block of the esplanade in front of the Hôtel des Invalides if he was moved on. The team of six men that Bowring was currently using on the job also had a big Toyota Land Cruiser parked handily in one of the side-streets.

Kelly, Gallagher and the three South Africans ambled and loitered in the open public space, watching the bearded priest stride in front of the pink mausoleum towards the great iron gates. They had already seen the tall, portly figure walking more slowly, a little ahead of Bowring.

It had occurred to the watchers that this exposed meeting place might have been chosen because the Arab did not have total confidence in Father Babbington. It seemed likely that there were others surveying this scene with interest.

Bowring caught up with the Arab just as they reached the corner of Boulevard de la Tour Maubourg and Avenue de la Motte Picquet. A group of three dark young men walked round the corner towards them. Abruptly, they turned behind Bowring. As they turned, a black Mercedes 500 limousine drew up to the kerb, its rear near-side door opened on to the pavement and Bowring was instantly and inevitably propelled through it.

Within seconds, Shalawi and his three young henchmen had climbed in after him. The doors were slammed and the car took off at a sprint, south-west down La Motte Picquet towards the École Militaire.

Haynes in the Renault van was already moving before Bowring was in the car. He stopped momentarily to let Kelly jump in beside him.

'Christ!' he hissed. 'They did that fucking neat.'

'They wouldn't have if the boss had wanted to put up a fight,' Kelly said. 'He reckoned that might happen – even if his guy Shalawi's for real.' He picked up the radio in front of him. 'I wonder how long Andy and those gorillas will take getting back to the Toyota.'

Haynes's eyes were fixed on the back of the Mercedes as it raced ahead of them. 'Try him in a moment. I hope to God they can catch us up. I'll need them to leap-frog behind these guys. Thank God there's plenty of traffic now.'

Despite the urgency in his voice, Haynes's manner and his driving were calm and competent. He knew exactly what he was doing, but he also knew that to do the job properly, he would need his back-up soon.

Kelly picked up the radio in front of him and tried to raise the Toyota. The Mercedes was heading up to the Porte de Sèvres before he got any response.

'Andy? Do you read me?'

'Yeah, sure. Where are you?'

'Getting on to the Périphérique, heading east. The traffic looks as though it's moving bloody slow. You might do better to cut down to the Porte d'Orléans. It'd be handy if you could get in front of them.'

'Right,' Gallagher's Glaswegian vowels rasped over the airwaves. 'I'll tell you when we're there. Shouldn't take long; this guy Heynrik drives like an orang-utan with a frontal lobotomy and a death wish.'

He cut out. Kelly grinned.

'Was that a good idea, sending him ahead?' Haynes asked. 'These people might come off before then.'

'They might, but we can still tell Andy to double back. My guess is they're heading for one of the autoroutes.'

Terry gazed at the five lanes of fuming traffic in front of him, moving in close order at no more than twenty miles an hour. 'We won't have any trouble as long as it's like this.'

The radio crackled into life a few minutes later as they crossed the Porte de Châtillon. 'We're at the Porte d'Orléans' – Gallagher said it like 'New Orleans' – 'Which way?'

'East,' Kelly said quickly. 'But try and let him catch up with you.'

Whatever had been causing the hold-up appeared to have cleared and, as if with a sigh of relief, the traffic surged forward once again.

'Shit!' Kelly said, gazing at the Mercedes ahead of them. 'They're pulling off towards the A6. Andy'll be on the Périphérique.'

Haynes shrugged his shoulders and followed the Mercedes.

'Hey,' Kelly shouted with a laugh. 'It's OK. There's the Toyota, look, about ten cars ahead of the Merc.' He looked at the map on his lap. 'That's bloody lucky. They couldn't have got on to the Périphérique if they'd wanted to.' He grabbed the radio and opened the channel. 'Andy?'

'Yeah. You arsehole. We've got filtered down to the motorway out to Orly.'

'I know. That's fine. Stay there. I can see you. You're only fifty yards ahead of the quarry. Keep your speed up. I'll tell you when to let them pass. Over and out.'

The black limousine containing Bowring and presumably at least five others settled in the inner lane of the motorway, remotely sandwiched by the Toyota and the Renault. It cruised past the spur to the airport and stayed in the stream of traffic heading south down the A6, the Lyons autoroute.

'I wonder where these geezers are taking him,' Haynes muttered.

'Shalawi told Bowring some associate had a house near Paris – he didn't say exactly where. The guy had to be careful, I suppose. If he's shopping this bunch of Muslim nutcases, he'll want to be bloody careful how he does it.'

'Yeah, and he'll need to check that Bowring's kosher first.'

Kelly laughed. 'I don't think kosher's the word.' He stared at the car ahead of them and their own back-up beyond it. 'I wonder if we'll have any trouble.'

'Maybe. Those Yarpies'll be handy.'

If there was trouble – Bowring had briefed them – Gallagher would be in command.

We'll see about that, Kelly had thought. But for the time being, he kept the thought to himself.

5

'Andy! They're getting off the autoroute,' Kelly snapped over the radio. The Mercedes had slowed and was pulling over to the right-hand lane. As Kelly spoke, the Toyota plunged across the following traffic to reach the exit road six cars ahead of their quarry.

'It's OK, Jack. We got them,' Gallagher replied calmly.

'Yeah. I can see. It looks as though they're going to Fontainebleau. Once they're committed, let them pass you, then stay behind them. We'll divert and come back to you.'

'Roger.'

The Mercedes was going fast down the old road, through the village of Ponthierry. It wasn't difficult for the South African driving the Toyota to let them pass convincingly. Once he had, both cars carried straight on, ignoring the right-hand fork to Fontainebleau, which Haynes took instead. Kelly got on the radio again.

'We've taken the N7. There are plenty of ways we can get back to you in a mile or two and leap-frog again. Let me know where you are.'

Haynes carried on towards the town. They were now in the thick of the ancient forest of dense conifer, oak and beech, broken by regular, ten-metre fire-breaks.

Gallagher reported the position of the Mercedes every minute or so, until he announced gleefully: 'I think we're getting there. They've turned into a village called Bois-le-Roi.' Then: 'They've turned up a track into the forest, about a quarter of a mile from the edge of the village, on the road towards Samois. Have you got that?'

'Sure,' Kelly said, as coolly as he could. 'We'll meet you at the crossroads between the two in ten minutes.'

He gave Haynes concise directions as they skirted Fontainebleau and headed back into the forest.

The Toyota was stationary in a parking place just short of the crossroads. It was a large clearing by the side of the road, with a few picnic tables around the edges. There were half a dozen other vehicles there and a couple of families sitting at the tables.

As Haynes drove the Renault in, Kelly spotted Gallagher sitting alone at one of the tables, reading a paper and smoking a cigarette. He had left the South Africans in the vehicle.

'You'd better talk to him,' Haynes said.

Kelly nodded, got out of the Renault and ambled over to the Scot, sat down opposite him and took out a pack of Gitanes.

'Hello, mate,' he said conversationally. 'We'd better sort out what we're going to do.'

'I've already decided,' Gallagher said. 'We'll have to go in.'

'Hang on,' Kelly said. 'Not so fast. It's much more likely these people are genuine. If they weren't, they'd have taken Bowring out in Amman.'

'Not necessarily,' Gallagher growled. 'If they're Sufuf Allah and they've sussed there's been a leak,

84

they'll want plenty of time to see what information they can extract. And as far as everyone else was concerned, Bowring was a Vatican envoy in Jordan. If he'd gone AWOL there, there'd have been a hell of a stink and they're not going to waste time with hostages. No one got enough from the last lot to make it worth while. Anyway, if we go in and they are genuine, no problem – we don't shoot.'

'That's too dangerous, Andy. Whoever they are, they'll assume we're hostile and shoot back. If they think we're on Bowring's side, they'll top him.'

'Listen, Kelly, if Shalawi isn't what he says he is, they'll kill Bowring anyway; that's why we should go in.'

'Look,' Kelly said, aware that he had to make some display of compromise. 'Whatever they are, Bowring's going to be alive for a few hours yet. Let's get to this place they've taken him and give it a full recce. We can make a better judgement then. For Christ's sake, Andy, there's no bloody point risking Bowring's life and ours for nothing.'

The Scot, though reluctant to admit it, knew Kelly had far more experience of hostage rescue than he had. He knew he must have spent hundreds, if not thousands, of hours developing his close-quarters battle skills in the 'Killing House' in Hereford. Besides, behind the verbal compromise, there was an uncompromising steeliness in the Liverpudlian's eyes.

'OK,' Gallagher said quietly, pulling two cigarettes from his packet and giving one to Kelly. 'We've got about four hours of daylight before we can go in anyway. We should be able to get some idea of their strength and set-up by then.'

With command of the operation now balanced

uneasily between them, Kelly and Gallagher made plans. Haynes was sent back into Fontainebleau to buy the largest-scale map of the area that he could. The best he could find was the IGN 1:50,000, which at least confirmed that there was a largish house with outbuildings, a quarter of a mile up the track where Gallagher had seen the Mercedes turn in. Between the road and the house, the track crossed a bridge over the branch railway line that ran to Fontainebleau and on down the Loing valley. Kelly had passed under this same line less than a mile back from the picnic area where they were now parked.

Kelly and Haynes took the Renault van – less noticeable than the Land Cruiser – up the lane towards Bois-le-Roi to see what they could from the road. The pine woods on either side were particularly dense and, according to the map, there were no other houses among them. The opening to the track – an ill-kept rubble drive – had no signs to announce the presence of the house at the end of it and looked little used. Haynes drove by slowly, while Kelly scrutinized every aspect of this approach to the house. Two hundred yards beyond the opening, within sight of the village, a van was parked beside a telegraph pole. At the top of the pole, an engineer in the overalls of the local telephone company was perched with the tools of his trade dangling from his belt.

Kelly tightened up. 'The overalls are right,' he said through clenched teeth, as if the man might be able to read his lips, 'but he's in a plain van.'

'Yeah, and he's some kind of darky.'

'There's plenty of Algerians work for the phone

company, but the van's definitely wrong. He's either on guard duty from the house, or someone else is staking out this place.'

'Shit!' Haynes hissed. 'That's going to make it tricky. What do you reckon?'

'Let's drive into the village and take the next road west of here. It runs about a quarter of a mile behind the back of the house.'

'Right,' Haynes nodded, taking orders from Kelly quite naturally. 'What was Andy's idea?' he asked as they wound through the narrow streets of the village.

'He wanted to go straight in, as if the boss was a hostage. I can see why he never made Selection at Hereford.'

'Yeah, he's a bit of a hot head, but he's a great scrapper.'

'I persuaded him we needed more info first, and darkness, to do the job properly. What we'll have to do now is an old-fashioned four-man patrol, though it's a bit of a bugger having to do it in a forest with Joe Public wandering about. If I'd known we were going to be doing this kind of thing, I'd have got a bit of training in.'

'The Yarpies'll know what they're doing,' Haynes pointed out.

Haynes had turned on to a main road that ran south to Fontainebleau. The forest on their left consisted of big old oaks and not much undergrowth, and Kelly peered between the tree trunks as the Renault followed an old van trundling sedately along. Looking at the map, he said: 'We must be behind the house about now; I can't see anyone, but there could be a hundred men in there for all I know.'

'There's another van parked up ahead,' Haynes said urgently.

Kelly swivelled his eyes forward. Besides the van was a small plastic screen of the type usually put round a hole in the road. 'I wonder what the hell they're pretending to do?'

'Electric,' Haynes said. 'Checking an underground cable.'

There were two men this time, both correctly clad, but again with a plain van.

'There could be half a dozen more in each of those vans,' Haynes said.

'Maybe,' Kelly nodded, 'but the problem's going to be finding out whose side they're on. If they're Shalawi's men keeping watch – and Shalawi is genuine – and we do them any damage, that could jeopardize the boss's chances.'

'Why?'

'They'll assume he's not what he says he is. They're not going to let him out alive then. Trouble is, if these other people are Sufuf Allah, and they're on to the fact that Shalawi's selling information about their plans, they'll take out everyone in the building if they can. From what the boss said, Shalawi's no soldier, and those lads who helped get him into the car didn't look up to much.' Kelly stared into the forest, not expecting to see a lot now. 'I'll have to check them out myself.'

Fifteen minutes later Kelly was jogging up the road towards the bogus electricians. He was wearing a pair of bright orange shorts, a St-Tropez T-shirt, flashy trainers and what appeared to be a Walkman. The two workmen they had seen were standing smoking at the back of the van. Kelly slowed to a walk, puffing hard, and grinned at the two dark-skinned, dark-eyed men. 'Have you guys got any water?' he asked in French with a strong southern accent to hide any hint of Englishness.

They looked back at him suspiciously. The elder of the two spoke in Arabic to his colleague. Despite the guttural Algerian accent, Kelly heard him say: 'It's all right. Give him some.'

The younger man walked round to the passenger door and came back with a bottle of Evian, which he handed to Kelly.

Kelly gulped eagerly at the water and gave it back gratefully, taking the chance as he lowered his head to glance through the back windows of the van. He couldn't see anyone else inside and the two Algerians hadn't made any noticeable effort to block the view. He wiped his mouth with the back of his hand, thanked them effusively, grinned again, and carried on at a slow jog along the edge of the road.

A mile further on, out of sight of the van, he stopped at an empty forester's lodge and walked a few yards into the dense woods behind it, listening for any human activity. Satisfied there was no one around, he unclipped the Walkman from his shorts and spoke quietly into it.

'Terry? Do you read me?'

'Sure,' the reply fuzzed through the headphones.

'Are you in Bois-le-Roi now?'

'Yeah.'

'I'll start running towards the village. Come out and pick me up. Have you found anywhere we can have a talk?'

'Yeah. There's a café in the square with a few tables outside. Andy and the others are sitting around having a beer like a bunch of tourists.'

'Fine. See you in a minute, then.'

The three South Africans, silent, surly men, didn't look like typical tourists but they didn't look out of place. They were dressed in jeans and T-shirts covered by light, loose anoraks. No one was taking any particular notice of them, for there were a lot of similarly clad, genuine walkers wandering through the village who had obviously spent the day tramping through the woods.

Kelly walked over to their table with a jovial greeting and some backslapping. He sat down on a spare chair and ordered a beer, then pulled the map from his pocket and spread it in front of him. As the waiter brought his drink, he described a fictional cross-country route he had just run.

When he judged they weren't going to be overheard by anyone, he said: 'OK. There's definitely a team in there. They're Algerians. Contract men, I'd say. I think it's very unlikely they're Shalawi's. I can't tell you how many there are. I've only seen three, but there could well be some already in the woods. They'll be waiting until it's dark, but like us they'll have wanted to do a recce first.' Kelly paused and looked at Gallagher. 'Do you want to hear what I think we should do?'

Gallagher shrugged. 'Sure. But this is a bloody stupid place to talk about it.'

'Six guys like us look a lot less conspicuous sitting around having a beer here than we would huddled in one of the cars out in the forest. If anyone comes near us, I'll change the subject. Try and look as though I'm telling you a dirty story.'

Haynes and the South Africans assumed inane expressions of amusement, while Gallagher put on a sulky grin.

Kelly laughed. 'OK,' he said quietly, leaning forward. 'We'll have to go in pairs – we can't risk a four-man patrol. We'll report back our progress to Terry, who'll stay here. Only take your nine-millies, and for God's sake, keep them out of sight. Don't use them unless someone's coming at you and you have to. If you come across anyone and they see you, you're just a walker – unless they start hostilities. It's very unlikely they will, because any shooting too early will bugger up whatever raid they've got planned.

'Basically, just don't get seen. You'll have to go as you are, though. You can't wander around in the daylight in OGs and camouflage. We'll approach the house from three start points.' He indicated them on the map. 'Andy and Hennie go down the side of the railway from the north, where the road crosses it just outside the village here. Jan and Willy start from the bridge on the lower road, near the picnic park. I'll go in alone from the forester's lodge there. Terry, you wait in the Toyota with the rest of the weapons. Jan and I will leave the van in the picnic place and regroup there after an hour, then come back up here. Terry, find somewhere discreet in the village where you can park and use the radio. Tell us where you are, and we'll come back to you and decide the best plan of attack. We should have some idea of what we're dealing with by then. How does that sound to you, Andy?'

'Fair enough. But we can't hang about. If these

others are going in, we've got to be right behind them.'

'Sure. It's five now. We'll meet back at the Toyota at six-thirty. Good luck.'

Kelly sat back. The rest of them laughed as if he'd just delivered the punchline. 'OK, let's go and get our gear.'

Hennie, who had barely spoken since he had joined the team three days before, and Gallagher walked west out of the village towards the railway line. Beneath their anoraks they each carried, in a shoulder holster, a 9mm Browning High Power handgun. Gallagher also carried a small rucksack. After they had crossed the railway bridge and turned off left on to a track leading across a field towards the forest, he patted the rucksack and grinned at Hennie.

'What you got in there, man?' the South African asked.

'My little Uzi, just in case we have a spot of bother before Kelly thinks.'

'Does Kelly know what he's doing?'

'Depends what you mean. If this was a properly sanctioned military operation, he'd probably be as experienced as anyone in the Regiment. He was a bloody good soldier; he was in Princes Gate and a couple of sieges in Belfast. But the rules are different in this freelance game and I'm not taking any chances.'

They were nearing the edge of the forest.

'How do you want to do this, man?' Hennie asked without a trace of anxiety.

'You follow the fence by the side of the railway embankment, about five yards in. I'll move parallel, ten yards further in and ten yards behind. I'll keep you in vision. If you see anyone, just stop. They might be blameless citizens. I'll get up to you. Keep me in sight.'

Hennie nodded brusquely. He'd been on hundreds of bush patrols in Namibia and Mozambique, in far more challenging and hostile conditions. He squeezed through the wire fence that bounded the field and slipped into the darkness of the forest.

Gallagher followed at the distance he'd specified. The undergrowth in this part of the forest was patchy, consisting of knotted clumps of fern and bramble interspersed with empty clearings edged with tall rhododendrons. Andy had some difficulty keeping his partner in view. The South African, despite the unsympathetic clothing he wore, slipped low, silent and barely visible from cover to cover.

Moving forward at the same rate, Gallagher stopped every few yards to listen and sweep the forest with his binoculars. Occasionally he had a clear line of vision a few hundred yards through the trees, and once he saw a family – parents and three small children – retreating towards the main road, a quarter of a mile to the west. They appeared relaxed and unhurried; he even caught a faint peal of laughter. They evidently hadn't seen anyone to worry them in that part of the forest. He watched them for a moment, then glanced ahead to his left to see Hennie stock still, crouched behind a broad beech trunk.

Hennie turned, saw Gallagher and beckoned.

With barely audible movements, the Scot took fifteen seconds to reach his partner. Hennie stabbed a forefinger across a clearing in front of them. The canopy of the forest was broken sufficiently to let in enough light for a small patch of tussocky grass to grow. Buried in a grassy dip in the shadow of a large rhododendron, Gallagher could just see a prostrate body in blue jeans and a white T-shirt. The man's head, if it was a man, was facing away from them, propped on his elbows, apparently watching something through the leathery leaves of the rhododendron. But from where they crouched, neither Gallagher nor Hennie could see what. They glanced a question at each other. Gallagher indicated that they should watch and wait for a few moments, and they both locked their eyes on to the motionless body while they felt for their Brownings.

For a quarter of a minute, the man didn't stir; then they caught a movement. The denim-clad buttocks were raised above the long grass, and slowly lowered again. The head disappeared from sight. The buttocks were raised and lowered again, then again.

Hennie nudged Gallagher and mouthed a breathless whisper. 'Christ, man! He's screwing!' he said with hypocritical disdain.

Gallagher grinned. 'Lucky bastard. We'll go round them. No point disturbing them — they might make a noise.'

Hennie nodded, and set off first, skirting to the left of the lovers. Gallagher waited, then took a route to their right. As he passed, not more than ten yards away, he caught sight of a naked female foot protruding from beneath the man's leg, and the motion, more vigorous now, drew a shrill squeak of pleasure. Gallagher felt an involuntary hardening of his own genitals, but ruefully turned away to concentrate on the way ahead. He and Hennie covered another two hundred yards without incident, sight or sound of anyone else.

Hennie stopped again. Gallagher came up to him to find they were confronted with a heavy chain-link fence some fifteen feet high and topped with rolled barbed wire. On the other side of it there was cultivated woodland and a glimpse through the ornamental trees of open parkland.

'This has got to be the perimeter of the place we're after. Let's check it twenty yards either way.'

Hennie turned east towards the railway line which had emerged from the cutting he'd been following and was now on a level with the grounds of the house. The fence took a right angle and continued as far as he could see alongside the railway track. There was a small humpbacked bridge about three hundred yards down the line, where the track up to the house crossed.

Gallagher had followed the fence to the west until he reached a right-angled corner at what must have been the rear of the property. They made their recce and met up again at the point where they had split. Gallagher pulled his radio from his rucksack and raised Haynes.

'We've reached a fence at the northern end of the property. Not too serious – burglar deterrent, I'd say; chain-link; cuttable; no sign of electrification. No trip-wires.'

'OK. The others have reached it too. Jack's sent Willy and Jan back to the Renault to come here. He's somewhere on the western perimeter waiting for you.'

Kelly's voice crackled in. 'Yeah,' he said quietly. 'I guess I'm halfway down. I've seen no sign of the enemy yet. Work your way round to join me and we'll check the rest of it.'

Hennie hugged the fence. Gallagher lagged ten yards behind and twenty feet out from it. After six minutes of silent progress, they reached Kelly.

'They've gone in,' Kelly whispered, nodding down the length of fence beyond them.

There was a straight cut, a yard high, where the severed edges of wire had been pushed in.

Hennie walked up and crouched at one side of the slit, peering at the ground in front of the opening. The vegetation had been scuffed aside, revealing a small patch of bare earth. He carefully pulled away a few straggling brambles, and after a moment he stood up.

'I can't tell for sure, but I doubt if there were more than four or five men through there.'

'That's all they'd need,' Kelly said, nodding, 'if they know what they're doing.'

He unclipped his radio.

'Terry. Change of plan. They've already gone in. I don't reckon they'll strike for another hour, when it's dark. But we'll have to be right behind them. Tell Jan and Willy to take the seven-thirty-threes and a dozen flash-bangs and go in two hundred yards either side of the road entrance. Tell them not to cross the bridge. They'll have to cut their way in instead. When they've got a clear view of the front flanks of the building, they should contact me on this frequency.'

'Roger,' Haynes said. 'What do you want me to do?'

'Get to the outskirts of the village on the lane down to Samois and I'll tell you when we need you.'

Bowring wasn't surprised to be ushered, without the option of refusing, into the big Mercedes when he met

Shalawi outside the Hôtel des Invalides. Had he been in Shalawi's place, he would have wanted to know for certain what he was dealing with before delivering information which would invite a death sentence if its source were discovered.

Inside the limousine, as it powered off down La Motte Picquet, passed the Champ de Mars and the Eiffel Tower, Bowring was confident that his six-man team wasn't far behind him.

'I'm sorry to use such impolite methods,' Shalawi said solicitously to him as they settled side by side on the deep rear seat of the car. 'But I would only be happy to pass to you the information I have in circumstances most favourable to me. And I'm sure you understand, we must satisfy ourselves as to your bona fides.'

Sitting opposite them on large, rear-facing dicky seats, were the three men who had hustled Bowring into the car. Two of them had been guarding the door of the hotel room in Amman where Bowring and Shalawi had first met. Once again, their hands were tucked into their jackets, making it clear that they both carried handguns. Bowring observed this, but was glad, on balance, that he had decided not to arm himself for this meeting. Beyond the guards, on the far side of a glass partition, a driver sat with another man beside him. Six to one, Bowring reflected: impossible odds.

'Naturally I understand,' he said. 'Do you have the documents we spoke about in Amman?'

'They will arrive at the house where we are going now, once we are satisfied that you will not . . . abuse the information they contain.'

'And what are they?'

'I have many interests, Father Babbington. Mainly I deal in commercial computers and office equipment. I also have an office services company in Beirut, which is very successful – software, faxing, desktop publishing, photocopying and so on. Since I have no wish to be involved in the disruptive elements who do not desire peace with our neighbours, I arranged that our photocopiers retain extra copies of everything that is processed by our offices, both internally and for outside clients. A trusted member of my staff looks through them every night for anything suspicious or of possible interest to me. It has been a surprisingly useful source of information to me.'

'I can see that it might be,' Bowring observed drily.

'I'm sure you'll agree just how useful when you see what I have for you. But that is all I am prepared to tell you about it for now.'

'I see,' Bowring said. 'What business do you carry on here in Paris?'

'I buy a lot of goods here. We have good trading relations with various computer companies, who have been quick and co-operative in adapting to our needs. Also, though I am reluctant to talk of such things with a man of peace like yourself, I have some interest in the ordnance trade.'

Bowring raised an eyebrow. 'That's a strange admission from a self-confessed dove.'

'Not so strange, Father Babbington, when you consider that peaceful settlements are seldom reached when one party in a dispute is armed, and the other is not.'

Bowring smiled and half turned to Shalawi. 'I had already concluded that you were a pragmatist rather than an idealist. That's good; I'd always rather deal with a cynic than a romantic.'

Shalawi laughed. 'You are right. I think we will get on very well.'

As the Mercedes joined the crawling traffic on the Périphérique, Bowring decided there was no point in asking where they were going. But when they turned off two exits later on to the southbound autoroute, he had the satisfaction of seeing the Toyota a few cars ahead of them.

Conversation for the rest of the journey was sporadic. Shalawi evidently felt that he'd said enough, and restricted himself to the occasional comment in Arabic to one of the young men opposite them.

They left the autoroute and took a road leading into the forest of Fontainebleau. Bowring made no comment until finally they turned up a weed-covered drive and crossed a fine ornamental wrought-iron bridge to draw up in front of a faded but still handsome eighteenth-century mansion.

'What a splendid house,' he remarked.

'It is quiet. We are seldom bothered here.'

Inside, the furnishings were disappointingly new and lacked taste, although they couldn't obscure the fine proportions of the reception rooms. Bowring was ushered into a large *salon* at the back of the house. The deep windows allowed views across simple rose beds, an ornamental lake and large lawns to a forest of grand old trees to the west.

'First of all, Father Babbington, I hope you'll forgive the formality of a search for weapons. This was not possible in the car, which is why, reluctantly, my young associates may have seemed rather menacing.'

Bowring opened his hands in a gesture of compliance. One of the guards frisked him quickly but thoroughly and grunted a negative at Shalawi, who smiled with boyish charm and said: 'Now may I offer you some refreshment? Coffee, mint tea?'

'Coffee, thank you.'

Shalawi gave a curt order to a male domestic who had appeared in the doorway.

'Will you excuse me for a few minutes,' Shalawi said affably. 'I have a few things to deal with.'

'Of course,' Bowring said. He hadn't been anticipating a short session with Shalawi. Several tours as military adviser to Britain's allies in the Gulf had accustomed him to the Arab penchant for procrastination.

Shalawi and his bodyguards left the room and the door closed behind them. Bowring walked to one of the windows and stood stroking his full, bogus beard, gazing at the splendid grounds without really noticing them. He was by now fairly convinced that Shalawi was what he said he was, at least as far as his own dealings with him were concerned. It was just possible that there was an elaborate and potentially very profitable hoax in the offing. Certainly Bowring now thought it likely that, whatever else his motives, Shalawi expected to make money from his information; his opting for the Vatican as a customer displayed shrewd judgement.

But in the seven days since their last meeting, Bowring had been frustrated by his inability to pin an identity on Shalawi. In the old days, when he still had a working relationship with the Deuxième REP and other French security forces, he could probably have got a line on his host from them. Now these doors were firmly closed to him, and he had to rely on a handful of friends in Whitehall giving guarded and increasingly sparing snippets of information. On Said Shalawi, they said, they had nothing to offer.

It was some time before Bowring heard the door open. He spun round to see the servant wordlessly bear a tray with coffee – French, not Arabic – to a table in the centre of the room and leave it there.

When the man had gone, Bowring poured a cup for himself and carried it back to the window. He peered at the forest beyond the gardens and wondered how his small troop was deployed. Although nominally Gallagher was in command, he had made it clear that there should be a sensible division of responsibility between him and the more experienced Kelly. He was aware that the Scot was a loner, but he judged that he had developed sufficient self-discipline now to work with a team if he had to. At the same time he had not forgotten that it had been an erstwhile lack of such control that had put paid to his selection for the Regiment. But, set against that, he had confidence in Kelly's charm and strength of personality.

He had no worries about Haynes's competence as controller of communications and logistics, and he was relieved that he and Kelly seemed to be getting on all right.

The South Africans he had brought in to add a bit of muscle if anything went wrong. It was probably an unnecessary precaution, but he would only have them on the payroll for a week.

Unconsciously, Bowring started to tap his foot. He was beginning to get impatient. The coffee pot was cold; the golden globe of the sun was dropping fast into the tops of the oaks beyond the park. There had been no sign of Shalawi or his aides for more than an hour. Although Bowring had trained himself to be patient, he was not by nature a patient man. He looked at his watch and turned his lips down with a sharp breath through clenched teeth. He wondered what the hell Shalawi was up to.

Decisively, he strode across to the double doors of the *salon*, opened them both and walked out into an oblong hall. His metal-tipped heels clicked loudly on the marble floor. A second later, two of the guards appeared, running down a broad flight of shallow stairs on his left. Both held Makarov 9mm automatics.

'What you want?' the first of them asked.

Bowring took no notice of the Russian pistols trained on him. 'I want to see Mr Shalawi.'

'Later. He still checking you.'

'Forgive me, Father Babbington,' Shalawi's voice boomed down from a gallery at the top of the stairs. His head came into view a moment later. He saw the guns and barked an order; the guards tucked them back into their jacket with surly obedience. Shalawi glided down the stairs towards Bowring. 'I'm afraid I've been having a little difficulty establishing your credentials. No doubt all will be confirmed very soon, but you do not appear on any of the normal diplomatic registers.'

'Naturally,' Bowring said easily, inwardly cursing Montefalco's lack of thoroughness. 'Mine is purely a temporary posting which wouldn't normally appear on the registers.'

'As I say, Father Babbington' – Shalawi was now standing a few feet in front of him, gazing at him with large, disingenuous brown eyes – 'I'm sure it will all be sorted out very soon. In the meantime, I'm sure you appreciate our need for caution.'

Bowring nodded. 'Yes, of course. But I really would like to get on with the business in hand.'

'It will be worth waiting for, I can assure you. Perhaps, in the meantime, you would like to eat? There is a good chef here. I will send him to take your order,' Shalawi added with finality. With a gracious but unequivocal gesture of his hand, he indicated that Bowring should go back into the *salon*.

Controlling his frustration, Bowring complied and the doors closed behind him once more.

6

Kelly, Gallagher and Hennie squeezed their way through the slit which had been cut in the fence by the Algerians.

Once through, the big South African scrutinized a mess of fresh tracks, and after a few moments he whispered: 'They split into two groups here – three that way, and two there.' He nodded left and right.

'OK, Andy, have you got any cam paint in your rucksack?' said Kelly.

Gallagher nodded.

'Good. Slap some on, both of you, and cover your heads. I'll have a look on the other side of this lot.'

Directly in front of them was a large spread of ornamental rhododendrons blocking any view into the park-like grounds beyond. Presumably, this was why the Algerians had decided to go in at that point. Kelly unknotted a camouflage net from his waist and wrapped it round his head. He dropped on to his belly and started to crawl like a lizard beneath the lower leaves of the overgrown bush.

He advanced with short, irregular movements to disguise any rhythm in the small, inevitable sounds of his progress through the dry leaves beneath the thick canopy. When he reached the far side of the bush, he wrapped the net across the lower half of his face and edged forward until he had a clear view through the gap between the lowest branches and the long grass. In the fast-fading light, he took a slow, careful look from left to right, registering as much detail as he could.

To his left, the lawns stretched some sixty yards north, and were planted with a few, isolated ornamental willows and birches. Beyond these, at ten o'clock, was a copse of half a dozen immature beeches. Between these and the house was a fine, spreading blue cedar whose lower branches swept gracefully to the ground, providing cover impenetrable to Kelly's vision. He noted it, and continued his sweep.

Forty yards in front of him was a lake about a hundred yards wide and fifty across. Beyond the lake, with a wide terrace between them, stood the house. It was a simple but elegant, classical eighteenth-century building whose rear elevation was designed to make the most of the grounds and the sunny westerly aspect.

Across the width of this front, a series of tall, unshuttered windows, reaching almost to the ground, reflected a faint pink from the last remains of daylight. There were no signs of any external guards covering these vulnerable entry points. It looked as though Shalawi and his men were unaware of any threat of outside interruptions to their meeting with Bowring.

Kelly swung his eyes to the right, stopping regularly to take a firm fix. By the south-west corner of the house stood a massive oak, much older than the house itself, whose vast, spreading limbs ended on one side barely a few feet from the south front.

To the south, the lawns ran into a big bank of tangled, neglected shrubs. Kelly estimated that the perimeter fence was no more than a few yards beyond them.

He listened to the birds making their final pre-roost calls. A blackbird burst into a sharp *chit-chit-chit* of warning from the woodland beyond the beeches to his left. He felt for his non-reflective, image-intensifying 10×50 binoculars and put them to his eyes. Magnifying any ambient light, they presented him with a scene almost as clear as day. He began a systematic search, starting with the foreground, stopping every few yards, alert for any signs of action or changes on each sweep.

On his third sweep, Kelly spotted a fleeting movement between the young beeches and the denser woodland beyond. Holding himself stock still so as not to miss anything, he kept his binoculars trained on the small stand of trees. He was rewarded a few seconds later by the sight of a man sprinting, bent low, from the woods to the isolated trees nearer the house. Scarcely breathing, Kelly waited to see if any others followed. After two minutes he concluded that he wasn't going to see anyone else. Either there were only two, or he'd missed one earlier. He thought they would then work their way closer to the house by way of the great blue cedar.

What lay along the north side of the house and beyond, Kelly couldn't see from where he was, but he guessed the raiders had identified a way of getting in close to the house from that side. He lowered his glasses. It was still light enough to detect movement with the naked eye; it would be at least twenty minutes before they went in.

Quickly, he backed through the bushes and emerged to find Gallagher and Hennie dark-camouflaged, their anoraks discarded and their T-shirts smeared with earth. Gallagher was bolting together the two parts of his Uzi sub-machine-gun.

Kelly shook his head. 'I suppose I ought to be glad you brought that.'

Gallagher grinned. 'I thought I might need it.'

'Not yet you don't. I've identified the position of at least two of the enemy. You and Hennie'll have to get round and take them out as quietly as you can. What else are you carrying?'

'Kukri, wire,' Gallagher answered.

'Hennie?'

'I've got my Russian knives,' the South African said smugly.

Kelly gave them the position of the beech trees and watched them disappear into the woods along the inside of the fence. He unclipped his walkie-talkie.

'Willy, Jan, do you read me?'

'Ya, Jack.'

'Give me your positions. You first, Willy.'

'I'm between the fence and a kind of garage block to the north-east of the house.'

'How far from the house?'

'Thirty yards at most.'

'OK. Get yourself due north of the house, in the closest cover you can. There may be two or three hostiles looking for a way in there. If you see any, deal with them. Try not to use a gun, but if you have to, keep it silenced. If you can't get to them before they go, tell us, then follow them in. If they reach Shalawi or the boss, be ready to bung in a couple of flash-bangs when I tell you.'

'OK.'

'Right, Jan, where are you?'

'I'm behind a little wall, about a hundred feet from the south-east corner of the house.'

'Can you see a massive oak, due west of you?'

'Sure.'

'Right. Head for that and get up it. You should be able to get on to the top of the house from it with your abseiling rope. But be careful, there are two more hostiles somewhere on that side of the house. I'm coming round that way, so I may get to them first. Keep this channel open. Over.'

Kelly took some camouflage paint from his rucksack and smeared streaks across his chin and cheekbones. He then shoved two thirteen-round Browning magazines into the rear pockets of his jeans and strapped his old SAS fighting knife to his belt.

The adrenalin was flowing free now he was getting close to the real action, but he hadn't any illusions about their position: as a result of his earlier tactics, they were almost certainly underarmed. As a unit, though, they weren't so badly off; the South Africans had their Colt Commandos and handguns, and Gallagher had his Uzi with four magazines. What was more, Kelly was sure that they still had surprise on their side.

Leaving his rucksack, he headed along the perimeter in the opposite direction to Gallagher and Hennie, stopping to listen every few yards. He reached the corner of the fence and headed east until he reckoned he was due south of the house. He worked his way through the thick shrubs to the edge of the open ground and parted the leaves.

Between him and the house he could just make out a low brick wall, level with the lawn on the far side –

a kind of small ha-ha. He guessed it must be the same wall from which Jan had reported his earlier position. Beyond the wall, at eleven o'clock, was the huge oak. He wondered if Jan was in position there yet but he couldn't risk using the radio. He lifted his binoculars to get a better view.

Hennie and Gallagher reached the woods behind the beech copse in time to see a figure flit across from it and disappear among the spreading branches of the blue cedar. Just then a distinct human noise, suggesting pressure on the lower colon, drifted from the beeches.

Gallagher drew his short battle kukri from its sheath, nudged Hennie and said, almost inaudibly: 'Let's go.'

Holding the broad-bladed knife in his right hand behind his back, he sprinted across the forty feet which separated him from the copse. He reached it before the two men standing behind the narrow trunks had fully registered the sound of his trainers swishing through the grass.

The nearest to him had just started to turn as the kukri flashed up a foot behind his head, and the perfectly balanced, curved blade descended with a soft crunch on to the nape of his bare neck. With a short gasp and a sigh, the Arab pitched forward and crumpled in front of him.

From his left, Gallagher saw the other man lunge at him. He dived over the motionless body in front of him, hit the ground and rolled on to his back. He winced as his Uzi caught him between the shoulder blades but started trying to pull the Browning from his shoulder holster. At the same time, he stuck one leg out at forty-five degrees to catch his assailant in the guts or genitals.

The Arab came down with all his weight on Gallagher's leg, twisting it viciously in its socket, and fell heavily beside him.

With the strength that only real danger can give, Gallagher lifted himself and wriggled his way out from under the man, ready for him to turn on him — until he saw a short, thick, steel handle protruding from the Algerian's back. The six-inch blade of Hennie's favourite toy — a Spetsnaz-issue MR-1 throwing knife — was buried in the heart beneath.

Gallagher saw Hennie looming over him, outlined against the dark, starry sky. The South African knelt down beside him and helped him to his feet. Gallagher leant for a moment against one of the slender beech trees, flexing his twisted leg. Hennie listened and gazed at the black lump of the cedar tree, fifty paces away, to catch any reaction to the small sounds of death their victims had produced.

In the sky above the forest, the last hint of sunset had gone, taking with it Bowring's view of the parkland outside. There remained only a faint, flickering reflection of the house lights on the lake. He turned away from the window, his patience ready to crack, when the doors to the *salon* were opened and Shalawi walked in with two of his guards.

'All seems well, Father Babbington. My courier will be here in an hour with the documents I have for you. Now, we will eat. Please, let me show you to our dining-room, where dinner is ready.'

Bowring had no appetite, but he was so glad his

wait was at an end that he was prepared to be agreeable about the idea of eating. Shalawi ushered him out of the room where he had spent the previous three hours, and into an adjoining room of almost the same size.

A large walnut table was laid with a number of cold dishes – stuffed vine leaves, olives, cheeses, small spicy sausages – and two places for diners on either side.

One of the surly young militiamen pulled out a chair for Bowring, who sat down gratefully.

The guards left, and Shalawi, sitting with his back to the black night outside, smiled across the table. 'I don't know about you, Father Babbington, but I am very hungry.'

He leant across to pick a stuffed vine leaf from one of the plates. Before it reached his large mouth, the room was filled with a deafening explosion followed by a blast of smoke and broken glass from the window behind him.

With pain and terror in his eyes, Shalawi turned, shards of glass and stains of crimson blood in his hair. Bowring registered this in the instant it took him to decide to dive under the table. He crawled around the central pedestal towards Shalawi, beyond whose chubby legs he saw two more pairs of legs, clad in boots and DPM fatigues.

He heard the throaty chatter of a Heckler and Koch MP5. Splintered holes appeared in the table top above him; the lower half of Shalawi's body became suddenly limp. Bowring carried on crawling towards the Arab, and when he reached him, he felt up the man's fat, lifeless legs to the waistband of his trousers. Feeling deftly inside Shalawi's loosely cut jacket, he searched for the pistol that he knew was concealed there.

He found the Beretta and removed it quickly, still watching the legs, running round the table now, kicking the fragments of glass. They knew he was there; they must have seen him through the uncurtained windows. The door from the hall burst open. There was the sound of a double-tap from a handgun, followed by two simultaneous bursts from the MP5s. Bowring exploited the distraction to get to the end of the table. Clutching the Beretta and smiling with grim resignation, he aimed just below the edge of the table at the first pair of legs coming towards him.

Kelly gazed through his binoculars and tightened up. Directly in front of him, no more than fifty feet away, two men crouched below the line of the wall. They both carried assault rifles whose manufacture Kelly couldn't identify. As he watched, one of them slowly raised his head above the wall. It looked as though they were going to go in any minute. He hoped to hell Gallagher and Hennie had had some luck with the three on the other side. And he wished he knew where Jan was; he couldn't have made it to the oak tree – these two would have seen him.

He sank back into the foliage and silently pulled his Browning from beneath his left arm. He was beginning to ease himself through the leaves with minimal sound when he heard the two Algerians scramble up and over the wall. Less concerned about noise now, he quickly pushed himself out and caught an outline of the two men running across the light cast on to the terrace from the windows of the house.

Kelly took an arc to his left, to keep out of range

of the light. He found himself beside the lake with a good view of the west front.

The two men were moving quickly along the terrace, checking each window as they went. Suddenly a third appeared, running silently from the other direction. They converged outside one of the windows, twenty feet from it, then ducked down and disappeared from view. Kelly guessed they were on the steps that led from the terrace to the lake's edge, a drop of no more then two or three feet.

A second later, the ragged thump of a fragmentation grenade shattered the silence of the garden. Two men jumped up, silhouetted against the window, and ran towards it. A second later, the deep *rat-at-at* of an MP5 resounded across the lake.

Kelly was already running round to the terrace. At the corner of the house he almost collided with Jan, who was sprinting up the east side of the building.

'Give me your rifle,' Kelly snapped. 'When we get to the window, chuck in a flash-bang, then follow me.'

Jan, still running, passed Kelly his Colt Commando, and unclipped a stun grenade from his belt.

They were still forty feet from the blown entry point when Kelly pulled up in the darkness between two windows. Two men had gone in; the third must have stayed by the lake to cover their exit.

A quick double-tap echoed from the house, followed by a sustained burst of fire.

Kelly peered towards the lake, into the darkness, trying to gauge the third man's position. But his attention was diverted by the sound of running up the terrace from the north end of the house. Three figures flashed past the light of the *salon* windows. A burst of fire on Kelly's left showed him what he was looking for. He swung round the M16 and spurted half a magazine at the point of fire. When he stopped, in the sudden silence, he heard a human gurgle and the clatter of a dropped weapon.

Jan didn't need telling. He ran on until he reached the shattered window at the same time as Gallagher and Willy. He threw in his stun grenade and jumped back to flatten himself against the wall. Kelly ran across and joined them. Cautiously at first, with weapons in the fire position, they turned into the window and jumped through, Kelly and Gallagher first, followed by Jan and Willy.

At the far end of the room, through the mist of the flash-bang, an Arab in a combat smock swung his automatic rifle towards Kelly. Before he'd completed his turn, he was shaking and jerking like a demented puppet as Kelly emptied the other half of the magazine into him.

As the burst of fire ended, the sharp, ugly sound of Gallagher's Uzi filled the room. Two Arab guards who had just run in waving their Makarovs pirouetted and tripped over their dead comrades in the doorway as they fell.

Kelly unclipped his empty magazine and flipped it over to insert the replacement, taped end to end with it. He looked around the room again. 'Where the fuck's Bowring?' he growled.

A hand appeared among the shattered contents of the dining-table. A second later, a face puntuated by a pair of hate-filled eyes raised itself, followed by the muzzle of an MP5.

Kelly was raising his own weapon when there was a single shot, and the dark, Semitic features slowly slid back out of sight. In their place, those of Father Babbington appeared, obscured by a large, crimson silk handkerchief. In his hand, Bowring held an automatic Beretta. The major glanced down, aimed and placed one more shot in his target.

Bowring looked back up at Gallagher and Kelly, who were now advancing into the room with their guns at the ready. 'There's a driver, and some domestic staff,' he snapped. 'They won't give you any trouble, but round them up and lock them away.'

Gallagher and Kelly went through to the hall while Bowring made his way to the shattered window. He stepped out to find Jan and Willy.

'Are there any enemy left out here?' he asked.

'I don't know,' Jan said. 'I guess we'd have heard by now.'

'Do you know how many there were?'

'Jack said five. There's one gone, over there, by the lake – after he did for Hennie.'

'There are only two inside. Get out into the dark and watch this window in case they come back.'

The two remaining South Africans nodded silently and melted into the night.

Bowring stepped back into the house and walked across the devastated room to the hall. He listened for a moment for sounds of Kelly and Gallagher dealing with the servants. There was some shouting from the north end of the house. With his Beretta in the fire position, he walked quickly along the corridor towards the commotion.

When he reached the kitchens, there were five men and two women sitting on the floor in a line along the wall. Gallagher was covering them with his Uzi while Kelly trussed them up.

'Jack, there were five. We've got two in the house, and one by the lake. What about the other two?'

Gallagher answered before Kelly could. 'Hennie and I, we done them outside. Did they get Hennie?'

'Yes,' Bowring said.

'Shit!'

'Where's Terry,' Bowring asked brusquely.

'With the Toyota in the village.'

'Give me your radio, for God's sake,' Bowring snapped. He activated the walkie-talkie. 'Terry, do you read me?'

'I read you, boss. You're back with us, then?'

'Only just. Hang on.' Bowring looked at Kelly. 'What's the best way out of here without using the drive?'

'Down the railway line to the bridge on the road to the south, just down from the car park where we RV'd earlier.'

Bowring crisply conveyed instructions to Haynes and snapped off the radio.

'Kelly, why the hell didn't you get him here before?'

'Too busy, boss. I didn't have time. We had to come in right behind those guys.'

'Well, the whole thing's a total fuck-up. They shot Shalawi before he'd told me anything and the papers he was going to give me hadn't even got here. Right, that'll do,' he said, looking at the terrified servants. 'Let's get out of here.'

Outside, Jan and Willy quickly stripped their dead comrade of weapons and anything else that might identify him, strapped him to a boulder from the rockery by the lake and waded in to carry him out to deeper water. As he sank, they ran down the south side of the house to catch up with the rest of the team.

Bowring and his four remaining men were swinging over the wrought-iron sides of the bridge across the railway line when they heard the wailing sirens of a convoy of police vehicles roaring up the drive from the road. They were running, a hundred and fifty yards down the track, as the first blue light flashed over the bridge.

Ten minutes later, streaming with sweat in the Land Cruiser, Haynes, Bowring and Kelly were heading for the bridge that crossed the Seine at Vulaines. Gallagher and the two South Africans were behind them in the van. No one felt much like talking until the river was between them and the carnage they had left behind.

Bowring, in the front seat beside Haynes, started to strip off his beard and clerical collar. 'Head north until we hit the A4 and we'll go into Paris from the east,' he said as he did so. 'They may put a block on the autoroute between Fontainebleau and Orly. We'll have to stop and get rid of our weapons and clean up. Keep your eyes open for somewhere, Terry.'

'OK, boss.'

Bowring turned to address Kelly. 'Not such a great result for your first operation with SOS.'

'Couldn't be helped, boss. That hit team had the place staked out before we got there. Someone must have got on to Shalawi in Amman.'

'Any idea who these men were?'

'Algerians; definitely not Palestinians.'

'Local contractors?'

'I should think so.'

'You didn't see the man who tailed me in Amman?'

'No. I should think any Sufuf Allah kept well out of the way.'

'You're right. I'm not blaming you for what happened.'

'At least we got you out of the shit, boss.'

'That one satisfactory aspect of the operation hadn't escaped me,' Bowring said quietly.

Next morning, the headlines of newspapers across the world bellowed conjecture at their readers. One aspect of the death of Beirut businessman Rashid al-Hussaini and his aides on which most of the media were agreed was that it was a strictly inter-Arab dispute.

Paul Lestienne brought the daily papers back to the house in Maisons-Laffitte for Bowring.

'As long as they don't decide to dredge the lake and find the South African, they won't be looking for any Europeans involved,' the Frenchman said.

Bowring grunted. 'That depends on what the servants tell them. Jack and Andy were blacked up, but they saw me.'

'You were totally unrecognizable.'

'Yes, but the driver might have realized I was English. Fortunately, he didn't hear any of my conversation with Shalawi – al-Hussaini, rather – because there was a partition between us in the car. Of course, they may say nothing. They may have been told not to by al-Hussaini's associates.'

'It says here that the house belonged to some anonymous import-export group who used it to entertain clients. People in the village, Bois-le-Roi, say they never saw anyone there, besides a gardener and a housekeeper.'

118

'We may get away with it,' Bowring shrugged, 'but it cost us a man, and we gained nothing.'

'Didn't al-Hussaini tell you *anything*?'

'No. They'd spent hours checking me out. Montefalco hadn't been thorough enough; Father Babbington wasn't on any of the diplomatic registers. I think I'd got through that though, and everything was going to be produced after dinner.'

'Any idea what he had?'

'Some schedules or notes of meeting – something like that brought into one of his offices in Beirut for photocopying. He told me that he had all the copiers in his Beirut bureaux rigged up to take extra copies for his own database. It was a smart move. People can be very careless about what they put in those machines; I know, I've done it myself from time to time when I've been away from my own offices. Nothing vital, of course, but things which could have compromised me.'

'But you saw nothing?'

'Nothing, but there's no doubt that something's up or they wouldn't have gone to these lengths to silence al-Hussaini and Father Babbington.' Bowring smiled. 'Although they don't know it, they've definitely done away with Father Babbington. Now all we have is a surveillance shot Kelly got of the Palestinian who tailed me in Amman. I may be able to get somewhere with that in London.'

'What's your next move, then?'

'I've paid off the two South Africans, though they could come in useful again, and I've sent Gallagher and Kelly back to Roquebrune to sort out ordnance with Bob Lyke. We've never had an assignment inside the UK that needed much armoury. I think it's far

more likely that Sufuf Allah will make their hit during
the British tour, not in India, and on the strength of
what happened yesterday I think we'll encounter some
serious opposition.'

7

Kelly was getting bored. He'd been in Ghent for three days and he'd visited every gallery, abbey and historic public building in the ancient city. He had been obeying orders. 'Just behave like a tourist until Bob contacts you,' Bowring had told him, and for the first couple of days he had enjoyed himself. Every few hours, though, he had been back to his hotel to see if there were any messages.

He spent the afternoon of the third day in the Schone Kunsten, wandering through chambers hung with fine old Flemish masters. He enjoyed the brilliant clarity of them; sixteenth-century moments frozen in time; details of the women's clothing and the soldiers' weapons. But after two hours he'd had enough. He walked back into his hotel for the twentieth time and nodded at the receptionist on the way up to his room.

'Mr Watson,' the girl called. 'There's a gentleman waiting for you in the bar.'

Kelly, buoyed with relief, nodded his thanks and changed direction.

Bob Lyke was sitting at a table with a cup of coffee in front of him, reading the *European*.

'Hello, how are you?' he greeted Kelly like an old friend. 'It's great to see you. I've only just got here, but I'd love to get out and take a squint at the Schone Kunsten before it closes.

Kelly sighed. 'Great.'

Outside he said: 'I've just spent the last two hours in there.'

'OK, we'll go and take a look at the Van Eycks in the cathedral, then. I'll update your orders on the way.'

The two men strolled like seasoned tourists through the medieval streets, unnoticed, unobtrusive, with cameras round their necks and guidebooks in their hands.

Lyke looked at his watch. 'I'm picking up the cash for our purchases from the bank in an hour, and the goods should be ready to collect from Bruges tomorrow. We've ordered more than we need for this job, but Piers thought we might as well use this trip to stock up on arms at HQ.'

'How much is there, then?'

'Quite a bit. M60s, MP5s, M16s, nine-millies, and SSG69s, ten of each and ten thousand rounds. A few Stingers, some PPG 66mm rocket-launchers and 40mm grenade-launchers.'

'How are we going to get that lot back to England?'

'Shouldn't be a problem. Michelle and Terry are bringing the boat over now; in fact, she should be in Ostend already. Take the 7.40 train there tomorrow; Andy will meet you from it. Rent a van and take it to one of the big chandlers down at the port. Buy twenty second-hand big polystyrene and plastic fenders – the scruffier the better. You'll find you can get some about three feet long, eight inch diameter – white to match the hull of the *Santa Laura*. Get a couple of dozen sheets of two-inch foam rubber from the street market. Gallagher should have arranged for you to pick up a stock of five-kilo catering tins of food and a

welding kit. I've already briefed him; he'll know what
to do with it all.'

'So why have I been hanging around here?'

'Preferable to you hanging around Ostend, and
I've got to give you the money. I'll do that back
at the hotel. Our supplier's OK, but if you make
it easy for him, he'll diddle us. I'll give you a list
of what we've ordered and the prices agreed, which
you must memorize then destroy before you leave in
the morning.'

'What's all this bloody marmalade and beans for?'
Kelly asked Gallagher. They were driving away from
a large cash-and-carry on the edge of the channel port
of Ostend. Stacked in the back of the Renault Traffic
van that Kelly had hired were eighteen catering tins
of assorted foods.

'To put the ammo in,' replied Gallagher.

'We won't need all that for ten thousand rounds,'
Kelly observed.

'Bob Lyke may be a bit of an old woman, but he's
a tight operator. He never lets you buy anything you
don't need. We'll only empty half of them for the
ammo; the rest we'll stack on top in the boat, in case
anyone comes on board for a snoop.'

'And the fenders are for the guns?'

'Aye, that's right.'

Kelly turned the van on to the old Bruges road.
Fifteen minutes later he pulled into a small yard full
of tractors, seeders, ploughs and a couple of rusty
combine harvesters. A large sign proclaimed that
these were the premises of Jan Bekkevoort, dealer
in agricultural machinery.

Kelly was still manoeuvring into a suitable parking

space when a small man in shirtsleeves and a grey-flannel cap walked over to them.

When Kelly turned off the motor, the little man poked his head into the window. 'Hello. Who are you?'

'Watson.'

'OK. Come in my office.'

Kelly and Gallagher climbed out and followed the Fleming into a small lock-up room tacked on to the side of a breeze-block-built warehouse.

'Are you Mr Bekkevoort?' Kelly asked.

'Of course I am,' the little man snapped. 'Have you got the money?'

Kelly nodded, but made no move to back up his claim.

'Well, let's see it.'

'When we've seen the merchandise,' Kelly said.

'Impossible. It's all crated up.'

'All the same, I'd like to check it all before I part with the money.'

Bekkevoort looked at the motionless blue eyes for a moment, then shrugged. 'It's not necessary. Do you think I cheat you?'

Kelly shook his head. 'Not now.'

'Come,' Bekkevoort said testily and led them out of the grimy office and in through a double door to the warehouse.

Four wooden packing crates, nailed up and strapped with steel banding, lay on the floor beside a fork-lift truck. In Flemish, the words 'Bekkevoort, Agricultural Machinery' were stencilled straight on to the wood.

Kelly tapped the closest to the door. 'Is this one of them?'

'No,' Bekkevoort shook his head hurriedly. 'The two behind.'

'Is that so?' Kelly gazed at him, nodding his head with a grin. 'Right. Open them up, then.'

With bad grace, Bekkevoort cut the steel band with a pair of shears and picked up a crowbar to prise off the lid of the first of the two boxes. He stood back to give Kelly and Gallagher a view of the contents.

The crates were packed with polystyrene bubbles in which nestled a number of packages swathed in black plastic. Gallagher picked up the top one and pulled out a Heckler and Koch MP5 wrapped again in soft, lightly oiled cloth. He quickly stripped down the sub-machine-gun and checked all the moving parts.

'It's fine,' he nodded at Kelly. 'In good nick.'

'Right. Let's do the rest.'

Bekkevoort lifted his eyebrows but didn't otherwise object. He showed no particular surprise, or contrition, when Gallagher and Kelly rejected ten of the sixty weapons.

'How long will it take to get replacements?' Kelly asked.

Bekkevoort heaved his shoulders. 'Tomorrow, next day.'

'Too late. You'll have to knock them off the bill.'

The arms merchant winced. Kelly suspected that Bekkevoort himself had been ripped off; but that was his problem.

Bekkevoort shouted a guttural summons into the back of the warehouse and a large, surly youth appeared.

Gallagher stood guard while the crates were repacked and resealed. Kelly went back to the office to settle up.

An hour later, they were parked among the noise and coming and going of a truckers' restaurant, where no one took any notice of the activity in the back of the van.

They dealt with the rocket-launchers first, reducing them to their smallest component parts, then the guns. They had made an incision in the top of the outer plastic skin of each of the fenders before peeling it off the polystyrene cylinder inside. Using a hot-wire cutter, they sliced the cylinders longitudinally and gouged out the inside, creating a tube with a one-inch skin.

Leaving the weapons wrapped in the soft cloth, they put each one into a black plastic bag, which they sealed before enveloping and taping it in a sheet of foam rubber. They packed all twenty fenders that Kelly had bought with the foam-rubber parcels, filling in the gaps with the polystyrene bubbles from Bekkevoort's crates.

With a plastic-welding kit, Gallagher neatly resealed the fender skins so that the earlier incisions were barely detectable among the scuffs and skid marks on the old fenders.

'Right,' he said when he had finished. 'The ammo. We need to take the bottom out of half these tins and get rid of the contents somewhere.'

'Where the hell do we chuck ten stone of baked beans,' Kelly laughed.

Each can, washed out and greased, accommodated about twelve hundred rounds – four deep – and weighed forty pounds. Gallagher re-welded the bases back on to the cans and he and Kelly stacked them the right way up, with the unopened tins on top.

'These things won't get past a real search,' Gallagher observed. 'But I reckon the chances of that are about a hundred to one.' He shrugged. 'I've taken bigger risks.'

Kelly nodded, unconcerned, and started stacking the fenders. Though heavier than they should have been, they seemed a better bet than the food tins.

They dumped the bags of jettisoned beans, marmalade and peas beside a pile of garbage outside the restaurant and headed back for Ostend.

Bowring's boat was berthed across the 'T' of a long pontoon, dominating the other craft in the yacht harbour beside the railway station in Ostend. Not for the first time during his two weeks of employment in Bowring's organization, Kelly was impressed.

The *Santa Laura* was an elegant, seventy-two-foot aluminium-hulled ketch, built twenty years before in one of Hamburg's leading boatyards. She had, Lyke had told Kelly, been twice round the world and broken a couple of Pacific race records earlier in her career. Now refitted internally to suit the kind of customers who could pay $10,000 a week, she spent half of each year paying for her keep with charters. Despite her vast sail area, she could be efficiently handled by a skipper and a crew of three.

Kelly drove the Renault van down to the harbour wall, sorry that he was going to miss out on the short trip across the Channel on board her this time; not least because, for this trip, the ostensible charterer of the *Santa Laura* was Michelle de Lassy. He didn't even see her in the ten minutes he and Gallagher spent alongside the marina. The skipper of the boat, an ex-marine, oversaw delivery of the stores and extra fenders and signed for them without a surplus word.

An hour later, leaning over the rails of the afternoon

car ferry, Kelly and Gallagher watched the yacht motor out of the harbour before heading off under sail into the calm, August waters of the Channel.

In Harwich, the two fit and tanned mercenaries strolled off the ship, each carrying a grip and genuine passport. A customs officer with a nose for incongruities identified them as the two most likely targets among a mundane bunch of passengers. He beckoned them over as they sauntered through the customs shed. Kelly was philosophical; at least he was clean. Gallagher scowled.

'No vehicle, then?' the official asked.

'That's pretty obvious,' Gallagher growled.

The customs man gave a nasty smile. 'Would you open your bags, please,' he said, nodding at the counter between them.

The Scot was fuming as they walked out of the shed half an hour later.

'Officious little bastard!'

He had just paid two hundred pounds' duty on his Rolex watch.

Kelly laughed. 'Listen, it was worth two hundred quid to see his disappointment. He was sure he was on to something with us.'

'Aye, well. He just pulled us at the wrong moment.'

They walked round the harbour to a van-rental company. A short while later, they were driving a small Luton-bodied lorry out of the port towards Colchester.

Next morning, after an unfamiliar, greasy English breakfast, Kelly and Gallagher sat in a café looking east up the River Crouch. They saw the *Santa Laura*'s sails across the flat, featureless landscape half an hour before they could see her hull.

They remained where they were as she berthed on the end of the pontoons, where, once again, she eclipsed the mass of smaller craft around her.

Kelly saw Michelle for the first time since he'd left Nice for Rome, standing at the bow of the boat as her crew neatly brought her in, under sail until the very last moment. When they were tied up, Michelle came ashore with the skipper and walked quickly up the pontoon to the harbourmaster's office. A few minutes later Haynes and the other crew members began to offload equipment – damaged sails, an Avon semi-rigid tender, a number of canvas grips, boxes of empty wine bottles and beer cans, a pile of large cans of peas, beans and marmalade, and twenty scuffed and battered fenders.

The crew came to the stone quay and collected small wire tolleys and took them back to fill them. After three trips each, the offloaded stores and equipment were piled on the quay ready for collection.

Michelle was walking back now with the skipper, who ran his eye over the unwanted stores and instructed one of his crew to stay with them until the van arrived. Meanwhile, the yacht was taking on fresh water and receiving a good swabbing-down.

Among all the activity in the busy marina on an August morning, it all looked very normal.

The two men watching in the café finished their third cup of coffee, got to their feet and walked to the car park where they had left the hired van. They drove down to the quay and crawled along until they were beside the stack of goods from the *Santa Laura*.

'Fenders first?' Kelly suggested.

'Aye.'

With the crewman, they had loaded all the fenders, the deflating Avon, and half the tins of food when they were approached by an official in white shirtsleeves and navy trousers. He stopped and looked inside the van, and then at the rest of the tins still to be loaded.

'Why are you taking off the food?'

Kelly, inside the van, picked up Gallagher's quick, uncomfortable twinge of anxiety.

The crewman answered. 'The skipper was trying to make a few extra bob on his food budget. He bought all this junk in Ostend, but the charterer won't touch it. It's all got to go back to our depot in Portsmouth. Christ knows what they'll do with it there,' he added with a laugh.

The customs man stepped forward, fishing a penknife from his pocket.

Kelly held his breath. The nine cans stuffed with 9mm and 7.62mm parabellum rounds were already on the van, along with five of those still containing what they purported to be. There were four undoctored cans still to be loaded.

The customs officer took a moment thinking about which can to go for. He reached into the van and put his hand on one which Kelly was just about to stack.

Kelly wasn't sure whether it contained baked beans or twelve hundred rounds of illegal ammunition.

'Let's have a look in this one.'

'Here, what are you going to do?' Gallagher asked indignantly. 'The stuff'll be worthless if you puncture the can.'

'It's not worth much anyway, is it? Seems a lot

of expense to be carting it all the way back to Portsmouth.'

The customs man slid the can across the ribbed metal floor of the van. Kelly noticed with a surge of relief that it didn't seem particularly heavy, but he still held his breath as the official stabbed a short, stout blade into the top and began to cut it away.

When he had cut a semicircle, he hooked back the top and revealed a pale-orange pool of baked-bean sauce. With a look of disappointment, he rolled up his right sleeve and plunged his hand into the unappealing quagmire. He felt around inside for a few moments and, evidently satisfied that no packages of heroin, cocaine or cannabis were floating inside, withdrew his hand with a shake of his head.

His hand and forearm dripped with the sauce. He tentatively licked a bit off, made a face, and asked if anyone had a cloth. Kelly promptly dived into his grip, already stowed in the van, and pulled out a dirty T-shirt. 'This any good?'

The man nodded and started to wipe himself clean. 'OK. You must have a very tight-fisted owner, wanting to save that muck, that's all I can say.'

Kelly didn't let his relief show until they were outside the perimeter of the marina.

'Shit! Bit fucking hairy, that.'

'Did you think so? I was enjoying myself,' Gallagher said, grinning broadly.

'Yeah, but you're a masochist. Right. Where's our RV with Michelle?'

'A wee village the other side of Chelmsford. There's a fella with a farm there, ex-Regiment. Mike Harding. Did you know him?'

'Sure. He was training when I first joined.'

He does a bit of close personal work for us, and a few other bits and pieces when Bowring needs him. He once came on a job in Australia. Getting on a bit, though. Too slow. He's got this farm; does a bit of horse dealing. It's pretty isolated, considering it's only thirty miles from London. We used it to lock up a fellow who was getting in the way on another job.'

'What's happening there?'

'We meet Michelle. She'll tell us.'

Kelly tried to detect any resentment in Gallagher's voice, but heard none. He glanced at the hard-nosed Scot.

'Have you ever worked an oppo with her?'

'Aye. We'd a wee job in Bosnia earlier this year.'

'The dam?'

Gallagher nodded. 'Something like that.'

'And what was she like?'

'Very fucking cool, man, I can tell you. I never saw a woman with less fear – not many men either.'

'How well do you know her?'

'If you mean, have I screwed her, the answer's no way. For a start, I don't fancy her that much. She's, you know, like, too good-looking. Good-looking women're always trouble. Besides, Bowring wouldn't stand for it.'

'Did he say so?'

'He wouldn't need to, man. You know what he's like; you know damn well he wouldn't approve of his soldiers screwing, even if they're the opposite sex.' Andy shrugged. 'So, if you want my advice, don't even think about it.'

'I'll try not to.' Kelly nodded reluctantly. 'She brought me in, you know.'

'Aye. She knows what Bowring's after, so she took

a good look and decided he'd want you. If she'd thought the other way, you'd never have known, would you?'

'No. He's managed to keep the whole SOS thing very quiet. It's amazing really. I never knew about it before.'

'It's in your contract: talk and you're out.'

'What about people who've been and gone?'

'There aren't many, and I don't know what he says to them before they go, but I can tell you, they're not interested in spreading the word.'

'But how does he get the jobs?'

'Through the agents, Dowson and Lestienne.'

'He seems to have made a lot of bread out of it.'

'He's made bloody millions, man, on all his businesses. He could pack up tomorrow and it wouldn't make any difference. That's what you've got to understand about Bowring; he does it because he likes doing it, and he likes doing it very well. He's got one of the best reputations in the business. Put it this way, if you're good enough for Bowring you're good enough for anybody.'

'But what does he spend his money on? He's not married or anything, is he?'

'No. I don't know what he does for women. But he spends all right. The only trouble is that everything he touches seems to make more money. Like that bloody boat. He bought it for nothing from an arms dealer's widow. Since he put it back in the water, he uses it when he wants, charters it the rest of the time, and he still comes out showing a profit. And you wait till you see HQ.'

Mike Harding had aged a lot since Kelly had last

seen him back in Hereford. He was still big and powerful – if anything his gut had expanded – and he'd allowed a grizzled grey beard to run riot across his big, square jaw.

He was standing in the centre of the three-sided Victorian brick-built farmyard into which Kelly had driven the van. He recognised Kelly at once, greeting him with coarse, cockney bonhomie. 'Well, bugger me old boots, it's Scouser Kelly. So we've got a boody Gulf War hero on the team now.'

Kelly took the hand Harding offered, and groaned as the man tried to crunch his knuckles into submission. With his free left hand, he gave a short hard jab to Harding's heavy stomach. Harding let out a loud 'oof', let go of Kelly's hand, and doubled up, grinning. 'Should've known better, shouldn't I?' he gasped.

'When you two have finished playing games,' Gallagher said, 'maybe you can tell us when Michelle's getting here.'

'She's on her way. My boy went to pick her up from Burnham. Then whatever you've got in that van has got to go into that horse trailer there.' Harding jerked a thumb at a standard double Rice box, hitched to a workaday Land Rover. 'Well, just the naughty bits. The rest you can leave here. I'll have a deal with the major on it.'

'I doubt it,' Gallagher said. 'Even you wouldn't take five-kilo cans of beans that had fallen off the back of a lorry.'

'Why not? The pigs'll eat 'em.'

'What about the marmalade?'

'I can give that to the quackers – ready-made duck and orange, eh?' Harding guffawed. 'Anyway, get a move on. I don't want your bloody illegal imports on the premises longer than need be. You can top the load up with hay.' He nodded at an open-fronted shed stacked high with bales. 'I'll get you a drink.'

He walked off, followed by three loping Dobermanns who had been sitting quietly behind him up until then.

Kelly unlocked the back of the van and rolled it up.

'He's got stuck into the good life, then,' he said to Gallagher.

The drive from the lane to the yard had taken them through a quarter of a mile of woodland and well-kept paddocks containing every conceivable equine type, from Shetland ponies to lumbering Shires. The house they had seen beyond the yard was a rambling timber-and-cob manor house set in front of a rush-fringed lake.

The Scot nodded. 'Aye, but like I say, he's gone a bit soft. Look how you creased him up.'

'I've creased up harder men than him,' Kelly said unemotionally.

Before they began transferring the weapons from the van to the horse trailer, they laid a row of hay bales on their sides along the outside edge of the floor of the box. Inside this lining they placed the fenders and the ammunition cans, bringing the load level with the bales. They filled up the rest of the trailer with hay until it would just protrude above the tailgate when they closed it.

As they finished, a new dark-blue Mercedes 500SL crunched down the drive and pulled into the yard. A young, beardless version of Mike Harding eased himself out of the driver's door, and Michelle got out of the other. Still wearing the denim shorts and deck shoes in which she had arrived on the yacht, she stretched her long, tanned legs ane walked over to them.

'Hello, boys,' she said with a smile, and not without an element of flirtatiousness. 'Is my hay all loaded up?'

'Aye,' Gallagher said. 'We were just about to put the ramp up.'

Michelle, carrying a small leather grip, walked over to see what they had done and nodded with approval at the barrier of bales around the bottom.

'OK,' she said. 'I've just got to change from sailing clothes to riding gear.' She walked towards an open stable door with her bag.

Mike Harding walked back into the yard carrying three cans of bitter. He saw the Mercedes and nodded at his son. 'All right, Jason?'

'No problem, Dad. No one came after us.'

'Good. If you want a drink, you'll have to get your own!'

Harding handed a can each to the other two, who pulled off the rings gratefully. When they had had a good mouthful, they heaved up the tailgate of the trailer and dropped the pins in to secure it. A few minutes later Michelle reappeared in a pair of well-worn jeans and a sweatshirt with 'I love Apaloosas' printed across the soft contours of her breasts. She had undone the loose bun in which her hair was usually gathered up and unexpectedly long tresses fell in golden profusion down her back and shoulders. She had generally contrived the appearance of a typical horsy Englishwoman, albeit an exceptionally attractive one.

Kelly looked at her appreciatively. 'Who the hell's Apaloosas?' he asked. 'I'm jealous.'

'A kind of spotty horse,' Michelle said, opening the driver's door of the Land Rover. 'You'll see. I keep one at HQ.' She climbed in and started the engine, then turned the trailer in the yard without any difficulty and drove off with a wave of her hand.

Harding gazed after her with admiration. 'She doesn't hang about, does she?' He turned his attention to the rest of the things that had been unloaded from the *Santa Laura*. 'Right, you better get the rest of this crap into the barn. Then drop the van off in London and hire an ordinary jam-jar, a Sierra or something like that, and get on down to Summerfold. Then I hope I don't see you for a while; I'm getting a bit too old for Bowring's capers.'

8

Gallagher drove the van into London. He and Kelly didn't speak much. Kelly bought a paper at a petrol station to see if there were any more reports on the incident in the Forest of Fontainebleau.

So far, at least as far as the reported accounts went, Kelly was relieved to find that no suggestion had yet been made of the involvement of European mercenaries. Which meant that the domestic staff must have kept quiet about them and no one had thought it necessary to dredge the lake holding Hennie's bulky corpse. The bogus telephone and electricity company vans had been found and traced to an Algerian gang in Marseilles. It was reported that those who hadn't been killed in the battle at the house had managed to escape down the railway track which ran alongside the grounds.

A week after the incident, Kelly still tingled at the memory of the action; he just hoped that Sufuf Allah didn't now decide to abandon their plans for the Pope's tour. In the meantime, he was looking forward to seeing the SOS set-up in England.

Summerfold House was a little over thirty miles from Hyde Park Corner; sited amid dense, mixed woodland on the southern slopes of Surrey's North Downs, it could have been a hundred miles from the capital.

Kelly and Gallagher didn't approach it by its long drive leading up from the small village that nestled at the foot of the hill. They went instead to The Hollies, a handsome early-Victorian villa, standing alone on the other side of the ridge behind Summerfold and about two miles from it by the deep, winding woodland lanes.

The Hollies was surrounded by neat paddocks. The original stable block and carriage house had been renovated and the presence of a horse trailer and a large fresh muck heap were evidence of the kind of equestrian activity which was popular among the wives and daughters of the commuters who lived in the area.

Gallagher parked the car and the two men walked round to the back door of the house. The door was open.

'Hello. Come in,' Michelle said from the light, airy kitchen. 'You're just in time for lunch.'

She was preparing a large French salad with *charcuterie*.

The two men helped her to carry the lunch and two bottles of Provençal *rosé* out to a flagstoned terrace behind the house.

As they ate, Michelle brought them up to date.

One of them – Gallagher – was to go with her to a small local horse show that afternoon. It was both her cover and her amusement to make an appearance at these events when she was in England; it decreased speculation about what else she might be doing, staying alone up at the isolated house.

Kelly was to go and see Bowring at Summerfold House.

'I'll show you the way before Andy and I go to the show,' said Michelle.

'No need. I've got the OS map,' Kelly said.

'But you're not going overland,' Michelle grinned.

After lunch, Michelle led Kelly down to the large, full-height cellars. 'Summerfold was built by a Victorian banker called Sir Joshua Bowring. Yes, some ancestor of the boss. Because the English were even more hypocritical in those days than they are now, if a man wanted to keep a mistress he had to be very discreet. Sir Joshua kept his mistress in this house for twenty years – but no one ever saw him come, or go.' Michelle pointed at a door set in the wall of the cellar. 'The tunnel is a mile long.' She walked to the door, turned a large iron key and swung it towards them.

Kelly shook his head in amazement. The cylindrical tunnel was brick-lined and over six feet high. Michelle fetched a torch from a hook at the bottom of the stairs and handed it to Kelly. 'It's a little damp in parts, but no real problems. I'll tell the major you'll be there in fifteen minutes.'

Kelly nodded, flicked on the torch and stepped into the tunnel. The door thudded shut behind him. He played a powerful beam along the dank brick cylinder as far as it would penetrate until it faded into black nothingness. With a shrug, he set off at a brisk walk, breathing in the damp but surprisingly fresh air.

The source of this air became apparent after he had walked for five minutes, when he suddenly came across a feeble shaft of light in the curved roof. He stopped under it and glanced up. Way above him, too far to judge the distance, was a small circle of light. The Victorian Bowring had evidently wanted to be sure he didn't reach his mistress short of breath.

Kelly thought of Bowring's set-up in France –

the passages and precautions that surrounded his operation there. At the house in Roquebrune, the other businesses provided cover for his mercenary soldiering; Kelly wondered how Bowring explained his presence to his neighbours in the depths of south-east England.

After the quarter of an hour that Michelle had predicted, Kelly found himself facing a large oak door with a big iron ring of a handle. He turned the handle and pushed. Contrary to his expectations, the door swung before him and he stepped into a brick-lined cavern some twenty feet square. In the middle of the room was the top of a well shaft a yard wide. Curious, he walked across and flashed his torch down the hole. An iron ladder disappeared down it, out of sight and no glimmer of reflection reached him from the depths.

Shining his torch around the rest of the vaulted cavern, he saw a door on the far side, similar to the one he had just opened.

Once again he turned the handle. This time, he was out of luck.

He looked around for some way of announcing his arrival to what he assumed was Summerfold House above, but there was nothing. The room was completely empty, featureless, except for the two doors and the well-head.

He put his ear to the inward door to see if he could hear anything and was rewarded with the sound of metal-tipped heels clicking on stone.

A moment later, after the sound of a key turning in a well-oiled lock, the door swung back and the cavern was filled with light from the passage beyond.

'Hello, Jack.' In the spotlight of Kelly's torch stood

141

Piers Bowring, in linen jacket and silk tie, with the hint of a smile on his face.

Kelly gave a short laugh. 'Hello, boss. What a way in!'

'More extravagant than you might think. It cost my great-great-great-uncle Joshua the equivalent of half a million to have it constructed, and keep it secret. And while you're here, I'll tell you about the other exit route.' He nodded at the well. 'The water level's over two hundred feet down, but at about a hundred feet there's another horizontal tunnel, only a quarter of a mile long, which comes out in an ice house behind the south lodge. Both exits have had their uses since I decided to move in here.' He gestured towards the door through which he had just come. 'Now, come on up.'

Kelly followed Bowring along a short corridor and a flight of stone steps up to another door to a higher level of cellarage. Bowring closed this door, and with scarcely any effort, swung a solid slab of brick wall across it, leaving it undetectable to any but the most thorough of searches. 'Apart from regular oiling, nothing's been done to that mechanism since it was built,' Bowring remarked, as they continued through a range of wine cellars, binned and labelled with dates from the previous century. Bowring stopped beside a stack of cobweb-covered bottles and picked one out. He blew a thick layer of dust from it. 'Calvados, 1892. Should be ready by now,' he said. 'We'll have some after dinner.'

They ascended another flight of stone stairs and emerged through a panelled mahogany door into a daylit hall. Bowring clicked his heels across a floor of patterned ochre and terracotta tiles to a wide, green-baize door which swung on double hinges into a larger, grander hall. A broad, extravagant staircase swept up beside them, and half a dozen elaborately architraved doorways gave off the hall. Bowring continued to the one nearest the front door and swung it open in front of Kelly, beckoning him in.

The afternoon sun flooded into the room through tall windows which allowed a stunning view over the tops of the trees across the lower Sussex hills to the South Downs beyond.

'That's a hell of a view,' Kelly said, aware that it must have been said many times before.

'Yes. If it hadn't been for the view, and its, ah, unusual means of access. I wouldn't have bought the place back. It had been out of the family for twenty years. A rock star whose name I forget bought it from my parents. Fortunately, he seems to have spent most of his time here in a drug-induced haze. Anyway, he never discovered the well room. Sadly, though, it's not a very beautiful house.'

'Well,' Kelly said, 'you can't have everything.'

'No, I suppose not,' Bowring mused, as if the idea hadn't occurred to him before.

Kelly looked around at the room – a library, perhaps twenty by thirty feet, with a large, black-marble fireplace and heavy mahogany furniture. The lights looked at least a hundred years old, and the only concession to modernity was a telephone on a large writing-table in the centre of the room.

Bowring picked up the phone and pressed a single number. 'Terry, Jack's here. Come down and we'll carry on with the briefing.' He cut the connection but didn't put the receiver down. 'Coffee, tea?'

'Coffee,' Kelly answered. He hadn't drunk English tea for over a year.

Bowring punched another key and ordered coffee, then waved Kelly towards a leather buttoned Empire chair and sat down at the table. 'Did you ever get round to reading your contract?' he asked abruptly.

Kelly nodded.

'You know then that the existence of this place, in so far as it has any connection with SOS, is inviolably secret.'

Kelly nodded again. He had got the hang of Bowring's *modus operandi* by now.

'You will only ever come to this place through The Hollies or, in certain circumstances, by the ice house. And unless you've told someone here that you're coming, you won't get as far as the well room. For your information, I occasionally entertain here, more to keep the local gossip under control than for my own enjoyment. I only keep two permanent staff, who are totally discreet. James, my butler, as well as knowing more than the average Master about wine, could probably outshoot you with a handgun.'

'Soldier?'

Bowring nodded. 'An old soldier.'

Haynes walked into the room. Although he had been aboard the *Santa Laura*, Kelly hadn't seen him either in Ostend or Burnham-on-Crouch. He nodded affably at Kelly. 'Hello, Jack. You found your way, then?' he grinned.

'Right,' Bowring said. 'We've got work to do. The Pope goes to India next week. From his itinerary, it's clear that the Indian security services have persuaded their government to restrict large-scale public appearances to a minimum. If I were planning a hit, I would dismiss any possibility of doing it on this trip. However, our clients will expect us to be around, to show that we're taking the job seriously. So, Jack, I want you and Gallagher to go over there and keep as close as you can, but don't make yourselves too damned obvious. Montefalco will be there, but you shouldn't contact him unless it's absolutely essential; in other words, if you think something really is going to happen.'

Bowring was interrupted by a knock on the door, followed by the entrance of a neat, quietly dressed, grey-haired woman in her mid-sixties. She was carrying a tray with coffee pot and cups.

'Ah, thank you, Nanny,' Bowring said with unexpected mildness. 'You haven't met Jack Kelly, one of our new recruits.'

The woman put the tray down on a side-table and looked steadily at Kelly for a few seconds, assessing and committing his face to memory.

'Jack, this is Miss MacFarlane, who had the misfortune to be my childhood nanny.'

Jack stood up and shook a small, firm hand. 'How are you?' he said.

'Very well, thank you,' she replied primly, making Jack aware that he was guilty of some small social misdemeanour in his approach. He could see why Bowring had such rigid, old-fashioned manners. 'Will Mr Kelly be staying in the house?' Miss MacFarlane asked.

'No,' Bowring answered. 'He'll be at The Hollies tonight.' This was the first Jack had heard about this arrangement; he was careful not to let his pleasure show.

Miss MacFarlane nodded brusquely and left the room.

When the door had closed behind her, Bowring said: 'If the situation arises, you can always leave any message with Nanny – however confidential. She is as much a part of SOS as any of you. Now, while you're away we'll be recceing every single venue on His Holiness's British tour. With Shalawi – al-Hussaini – gone, we're not going to get any more information from that source, so we'll have to do the job by tactical pre-emption. In other words, we'll have to second-guess them, and hope they're good enough to choose the right places.'

Haynes made a face. 'I still think it's too wide open, boss. Frankly, with so little intelligence there's too many places to look.'

'We have some intelligence,' Bowring said impatiently. 'We have a photograph of one of their men on the ground in Amman. It's not much, but it's a start. I've given it to an old colleague in counter-terrorism. They'll spot him if he comes in – at least they bloody well should. And I think I can persuade them to leave him alone.'

'Without letting on what you know?' Kelly asked.

'Don't worry about that. By the time you get back from India, we'll have produced a short-list of likely hit spots. Michelle will be covering the Pope's visit for a news agency in Nice. She's got her press credentials; she'll be able to do a lot of the close reconnaissance while she's doing her local colour pieces.'

Kelly nodded. 'With a camera?'

'Yes. And Terry will be producing all the scale maps and layouts that we'll need.'

It was, as Haynes had said, a very wide brief, but

Kelly accepted Bowring's proposition that the right hit spots would be fairly predictable. 'Boss, what concerns me is that there won't be enough of us,' he said, however.

'There'll be five of us on the ground. If we get the right spot, we don't need to be more; if we get the wrong one, it wouldn't make any difference if we were a whole squadron. And if Sufuf Allah get on to us, we'll be severely hampered; the fewer of us there are, the less chance there is of that happening.'

'But they knew you met al-Hussaini in Amman,' Kelly said.

'True, but they know they've silenced him, and they're not going to see Father Babbington again. Of course, it's quite possible they may abandon the whole op.' Bowring shrugged. 'We'd still get our performance bonus, but I'd feel we'd earned it rather too easily.'

'But you nearly got your head blown off in Fontainebleau,' Kelly said with a grim laugh.

'It'd take more than a pair of trigger-happy Algerians waving MP5s to blow my head off,' Bowring replied unemphatically. 'Now tomorrow, Jack, I want you to familiarize yourself with the anti-intrusion devices around the grounds here. Obviously I've had to keep them fairly discreet.'

'What's the area?'

'About twenty-five acres. Apart from four acres of semi-formal garden, the rest is woodland. There's a perfectly normal chain-link perimeter fence – six feet high and unprotected on top. A yard in from that is a disturbance sensor wire. It gets triggered from time to time by deer, foxes and badgers, but the circuit's complete at the moment. A hundred feet inside the fence we've got a series of magnetic and seismic intrusion detectors. There are also concealed CCTV cameras with image-intensifying filters sited in six old oaks, and four fitted on the corners of the house.' Bowring shrugged and spread his hands. 'It's not ideal, but anything more elaborate would arouse suspicions; one of my boundaries is with a patch of National Trust woodland and there's always someone pottering around in there. Up till now I've had no cause to feel this place was a target, but then we seldom operate in the UK – nothing serious anyway. I want to take a few more precautions, in the unlikely event that Sufuf Allah latch on to us. I've got a couple of dozen American acoustic buoys on FM transmitters that need siting. You could do that while you're checking the others.'

'Have you got maps of the lay-out?' Kelly asked.

'Yes. You can have those so you can get on with it tomorrow and do a few checks with Terry.'

'OK, boss. When do we go to India?'

'At the end of the week. You'll need to arrive a couple of days before the Pope and run checks on his accommodation; you'll have Vatican IDs for that. But, whatever you do, keep a low profile.'

Bowring spent another hour with Kelly and Haynes looking at the Pope's British itinerary, highlighting the places to be recced first. Later, Bowring took them to his billiard-room and left them there with a well-stocked drinks tray and instructions to enjoy themselves for a couple of hours. A series of fiercely competitive games of snooker, accompanied by a post-mortem of the Fontainebleau fiasco occupied them until Bowring reappeared to tell them that dinner was ready.

James served the meal for them at a dining-table that would have seated twenty. Kelly watched him, impressed by what Bowring had told him of this suave, silent man's shooting prowess. He would never have credited it were it not that Bowring seemed to have a natural skill at attracting this unexpectedly multi-talented type of person to his entourage. Even Nanny looked as though she could handle herself in a fight, as well as issue instructions on the correct way to eat peas.

After dinner and some glasses of the ancient, silky calvados, Bowring rang The Hollies, and Kelly was seen off through the concealed door, down into the well room. Fifteen minutes later, Michelle was pulling back the door at the other end of the tunnel. She let him into the cellar, and bolted the door again.

Upstairs, she and Gallagher had just finished dinner.

It was only ten o'clock, and Gallagher suggested that they should go out for a drink.

Michelle shook her head. 'But you two go. Just don't tell anyone where you're staying or let them see you coming back here.'

Gallagher drove the car through a circuitous route of tiny lanes to a village pub called the Thomas à Becket. It was Saturday night and the pub was fairly busy, but they found a corner to drink their pints in relative privacy.

'Well,' Gallagher asked. 'What did you think of HQ?'

'It's a hell of a set-up, but I just wonder what Bowring does with himself up there all the time.'

'He works,' the Glaswegian said simply. 'He's got fingers in umpteen pies and he likes to keep up to date with all of them. He's got no interest in other people, and even though you might think he's sort of charming on the surface, you'll find he only ever talks about his own projects.'

'I suppose so,' Kelly agreed. 'He was always like that in the squadron, but he's even got his old nanny working for him up there.'

'She wouldn't be there if she wasn't bloody useful to him,' Gallagher said. 'He's a very hard man, is Bowring,' he added with obvious admiration. 'You could drag the Gorbals and not find a harder one. It's his English gent manners that fool most people, but I can tell you, they don't mean a thing. If you stopped being useful to him, he'd sling you out – or kill you. That's why I like him – I know where I am with him.'

'What do you think about this job we're on now?'

'To tell you the truth, I think it stinks. We don't know half enough.'

Kelly nodded. 'Just what Terry was saying, but the boss seems to think we can do it.'

'He always does; and usually he's right,' Gallagher said with a shrug. 'That's why I'm still here.'

'Do you ever feel you want to jack this lot in? You know, marry and settle down?'

'No way. I tried. Hated it. I couldn't stick knowing what was going to happen every day, nothing to get the adrenalin going. How about you?'

'I was married, for a year or so, but she couldn't take it. I was still in the Regiment, you know, going off for a few weeks here and a few months there. She just couldn't hack it – went off with a bloody tractor salesman. She's still got a car of mine. I'll have to go back to Hereford and sort it out sometime. I bought one of those Morgan cars; they make them near there, and I've never been back to collect it. I couldn't face having to be nice to the new husband.'

Gallagher nodded and took a long pull at his pint. When he spoke again, it was not of their personal problems. 'Did Bowring tell you he's sending us to India?'

'Yes. In four or five days.'

'That's what Michelle said, but he hasn't told me; I guess he will tomorrow, but I'm going to tell him he's crazy. If we have to work in close to the Pope, we'll get spotted. Even if these Sufuf Allah don't try anything in India, they're more than likely going to be there checking out personal security arrangements. If they see us in England after that, they'll be on to us.'

'But they'd just think we were part of the Pope's team.'

'Look, they'd know our faces, and we'd lose most of our advantage. I think it's crazy for us to go.'

'Will Bowring listen to you?'

'Sure, if you back me up.'

They were drinking coffee on the terrace early next morning when James arrived via the tunnel. He was dressed like the gamekeeper of a large estate. He introduced himself this time, with the voice of a north country vicar, as Jim Mason.

'I've come for the weapons. I'll be driving them straight up to the house in the horse trailer. Mr Kelly, when you get up there, you're to help me unload them and put them in the gunroom.'

Kelly suggested the butler sit and join them for a

cup of coffee, but he declined, got the keys to the Land Rover from Michelle and drove away.

'Unfriendly bugger,' Gallagher snorted as they listened to the vehicle rumbling away.

Kelly didn't see Bowring when he arrived at Summerfold House but James was waiting for him. The trailer was backed up to a door at the rear of the house that had been designed for the delivery of coal straight into the cellars down a well-worn wooden chute. James showed Kelly down the stairs from the back hall, then turned into a small passage at the entrance to the wine vaults.

The coal cellar, redundant since oil-fired boilers had been installed, contained only a supply of logs for the open fires. Beyond it, through a sturdy oak door similar to the one which gave into the well room, was the gunroom. This was no gunroom in the country-house sense: the only shotguns it contained were pump-action Remingtons and Franchi SPAS 15s. It was lined with concrete and steel, and the inside of the door was a solid iron sheet. The racks which lined two walls were designed to hold over a hundred weapons of various types and sizes and a two-ton walk-in safe contained ammunition, land-mines and 66mm rockets.

By the time James had passed down Kelly's recent purchases from Bekkevoort in Bruges, the racks were full. When they had finished, they made a complete inventory of what was now a comprehensive arsenal of light assault hardware. Upstairs, the butler gave Kelly the acoustic buoys and charts of the grounds as if they were a gift from the Queen.

Dressed in a Barbour and flat tweed cap courtesy of the house, Kelly set off for the woods to carry out Bowring's instructions of the evening before. He left by the back of the house and crossed a large expanse of lawn, surrounded by an extravagant display of huge azaleas. Dotted about the garden were ornamental trees of the varieties favoured in mid-Victorian times – monkey-puzzles, Douglas firs and soaring Wellingtonias. Beyond these, the woods were thick with well-established oak, ash, beech and conifer, with a dense undergrowth of laurel and bracken which liked the acid, sandy soil. Once in the woods, Kelly called up Haynes on his walkie-talkie handset.

'OK, Terry, you should be getting me on one of the mini seismic detectors now, if I'm where I think I am.'

'Getting you faintly,' Haynes came back.

The AN/GSQ-154 miniature seismic intrusion detector would pick him up from about eighty feet in this sort of terrain. Kelly took a bearing and headed deeper into the woods until Haynes crackled over the radio that he had him good and strong. They repeated the exercise with the other seismics, and then moved on to the MAGID Model T4 DT-516/GSQs, magnetic intrusion detectors that would pick up a human carrying weapons from about ten feet.

When they had located and checked all of the detectors, Kelly turned his attention to the tiny thread of wire that ran inside the perimeter fence. He cut and then repaired it in four places, having got a positive check that the breaks in the circuit were registering.

As he had made his rounds of the existing equipment, he made notes of sites for his bagful of US Army acoustic buoys. For the most part he suspended them, out of sight, from the branches of trees, ten to twelve feet above the ground with about two hundred yards between each. Their small, integral FM radio transmitters would relay any sounds within normal human hearing.

When he had placed and checked them all with Haynes, he was satisfied that, provided the receivers were adequately monitored, intruders by any route would be detected, even if the CCTV missed them.

As it happened, Haynes had reported Kelly within sight of the sweep of the cameras in the woods for about twenty per cent of the time. The cameras on the house would take in a close approach from almost all directions.

Back in the communications room in the attic, Kelly and Haynes ran through the receiving ends of the systems, most of which Kelly had previously used in some form. Gallagher, who had been summoned up the tunnel with him that morning, hadn't been seen since his arrival. Eventually he too came up to the communications room.

'The boss wants to see you,' he said to Kelly. 'He's in the library.'

Kelly nosed the Land Rover through the sunken lanes, down to the main road running westwards to Guildford. The steady rush of weekend traffic struck him as somehow unreal after the seclusion of Summerfold House and the quiet emptiness of the wooded hills only a mile or so behind him.

He turned, heading towards Guildford, the M4 and finally Hereford.

India was off.

Bowring had listened to Gallagher and agreed,

without any resentment, almost as if he'd been expecting the objections. Perhaps he had; perhaps he liked to see how much constructive input his team could provide. He had already arranged to bring two men back from El Salvador for a quick briefing in the UK before setting off to keep close to the Pope in the subcontinent.

Kelly, glad of the chance to follow up his vague plan of two evenings before, had been dispatched to stock up on clothing and equipment from a large army surplus store close to the Regiment's home base. Bowring had agreed to give him an extra day to sort out his own business while he was there.

Walking into a bar in Hereford a few hours later, tanned, fit, obviously in work, Kelly was greeted jovially by those of his old colleagues who were there. He'd fought beside several of them and the bond that that creates is never completely broken.

He'd booked into a small hotel in the town and spent the evening grumbling good-humouredly to his mates about the boredom of most of the work he'd been doing since leaving Hereford. But he said nothing about Major Piers Bowring and Special Operations Services S.A.

At the same time he kept his ears open for news of other old colleagues, in case Bowring needed more recruits in the future. He left late, with an invitation to come to the Sergeants' Mess the following day.

In the bright, cloudless morning, the ridge of the Black Mountains, twenty-five miles west of Hereford, and the steep bluff of Gospel Pass above Hay-on-Wye, stood out clear against a blue sky. It was Kelly's first sight of the Welsh mountains for three years. They reminded him sharply of his arrival in Hereford as a twenty-three-year-old, determined to show anyone and everyone that he had what it took.

Now here he was fifteen years on, with nothing to prove, reluctant even to talk about what he was doing; yet he preferred it that way.

He smiled at the warm, familiar landscape as he drove the khaki Land Rover west out of Hereford towards the village of Eardisley.

Twenty minutes later, he slowed down as he approached a garage forecourt where half a dozen new tractors stood with a gleam on their red paint which wouldn't last a week once they had found a buyer. His ex-wife Susan and her husband, Will, lived in a large, timber-framed house behind the garage. In the garden, Kelly could make out the signs of a small child's presence – splashes of red and yellow plastic on the lawn; tiny clothes on the washing-line. He hadn't heard about a baby. By choice, he'd heard nothing in the two years since his divorce had become absolute.

Now this evidence of fertility in the woman he had, he supposed, once loved, gave him a sharp rush of sadness. But, setting his jaw, he came to a halt, reversed the Land Rover into a track and drove slowly back to the garage.

Will saw him, recognized him at once, and came nervously out of his glass-fronted office.

Kelly turned the motor off, jumped down from the dusty vehicle and waited for the chubby, red-faced tractor dealer to walk up to him.

'Hello, Jack. I didn't know you were coming.'

'Nor did I until this morning.'

'What . . . er, what did you want?'

'Just to see how you were getting on.'

'Oh, we're pretty good. Business hasn't been so bad, considering. Better than it was, anyway.'

'Glad to hear it. I see you've been building on to the house. Susan must be happy about that.'

'She is.' Will shut his mouth, uncertain what to say next, unwilling to show how little he wanted this hard, almost legendary, samurai to stay, not relishing any comparisons his wife might later make between them.

'Is she in, then?'

'Yeah. With the boy.'

'It's a boy, is it? No one told me.'

'Well, I don't suppose Sue thought you'd be interested. Anyway, she wouldn't know where to find you.'

Kelly nodded and started to walk towards the back of the garage building. 'I'll go and find her. There was something I wanted to talk to her about.'

Will waddled along beside him. 'What's that, then?'

'It's OK. I'll talk to her about it.'

Will looked worried, dropped his shoulders and fell behind.

Kelly strode casually across a patchy new lawn towards a paddling-pool where he could see Susan leaning over, splashing the child and laughing with him.

'Hello, Susan.'

She straightened her back and spun round. Her big brown eyes showed gladness, sadness and remorse.

'Jack! What are you doing here?' There was a tremor to her soft, Herefordshire voice. Guilt? Excitement? Kelly couldn't tell.

'I was in Hereford. I thought I'd drop in and see

you.' He smiled. Susan relaxed; she looked better now than when she'd walked out on him. 'And I thought I'd pick up the Morgan. I quite fancy it where I'm working down in the South of France.'

Susan's eyes dropped; she appeared to be studying the hem of her short cotton skirt. 'You . . . you'll have to talk to Will about that.'

'Why? What's it got to do with Will?'

'You talk to him,' Susan said, meeting Kelly's eye for a second.

'OK. I will in a moment. Aren't you going to introduce me to your son?'

Susan turned back to the small boy, splashing eagerly in the pool. She bent down and picked him up, holding his wet little body to her tight cotton T-shirt. 'This is Bobby. Bobby, say hello to Jack.'

The boy glanced at Kelly without much interest before turning back to his mother's breast. Susan gave an embarrassed laugh. 'I haven't really started teaching him his manners yet.'

Kelly looked at Susan's nipple, standing proud beneath the damp T-shirt. He thought about the baby sucking it. 'How old is he, then?'

'Just eighteen months.'

'He looks well.'

'So do you, Jack. Too well, almost. What you been doing?'

'This and that. Nothing very exciting.'

'Doing all right, then?'

'Making a few bob.'

'Have you got yourself a house yet, then?'

Kelly shook his head.

Susan looked relieved.

'Well, would you like a coffee or something?'

'No thanks. I haven't got a lot of time. I'd better go and talk to your husband about my car, if you won't.'

'Right. Well, I'll see you another time, then, maybe.'

'Maybe. OK, love?'

Kelly looked at her for a moment, gave her a quick wink and turned abruptly to walk back to the garage.

Will was talking to a farmer who had drawn up in an old pick-up. He looked round quickly when he heard Kelly coming and began to jiggle from foot to foot. 'I'll have to talk to this gentleman who's been waiting to see me, Mr Pugh. You come tomorrow and we'll sort it out, all right?'

The farmer nodded warily, then started his engine and drove slowly away.

'Where's the Morgan, then, Will?'

'The Morgan?'

'Yes, Will, the fucking Morgan. I left it with Susan for her to look after until I could pick it up. Well, I've come to pick it up, but she says I should talk to you about it. So, where is it?'

Will's russet features glowed.

'It's . . . it's not here at the moment.'

'Where is it, then?'

Will gulped. 'It's gone.'

'What do you mean, it's gone? You mean it's been nicked, or what?'

'Well, to tell you the truth, when you never came and picked it up, Susan thought you weren't ever going to. So . . . she asked me to sell it.'

Kelly wanted to laugh at the man's discomfort. But he didn't. His eyes narrowed.

159

'So you sold it, did you? How did you deal with the logbook?'

'I signed it for you.'

'You forged my signature on the change-of-owner slip?'

Will bit his lower lip and nodded.

'Oh well. It's not the end of the world. How much did you get for it?'

'Fifteen grand,' Will said quickly.

Kelly looked at him without speaking for a moment. Then he shook his head once. 'I think we'd better talk about this inside.'

Will seemed suddenly paralysed.

'In your office, Will,' Kelly hissed.

The tractor dealer forced his legs to carry him through the showroom doors, past a pair of newish Land Rovers and into his office.

Kelly followed.

'Now,' he said. 'That Morgan was brand-new. It cost me eighteen grand, but you can get a premium of three or four on the list price. So, tell me again: how much did you get for it?'

'Fifteen, I promise you, Jack,' Will whined.

Kelly was facing him now, with barely a foot between them, looking him straight in the eyes. He smiled as he slowly drew his right fist back beside his waist.

Will saw it; his fleshy face twitched; frozen with fear, he couldn't move. Kelly's fist came forward like a steam hammer and buried itself in Will's flabby guts.

Will gasped and coughed, stumbling forward as Kelly's left fist caught him full on the nose.

Kelly stepped back and let him collapse on to the

floor in front of him. He got down on his haunches to continue their conversation.

'How much did you get for it?' he asked again.

Will coughed and groaned before lifting his head a few inches off the ground, leaving a splash of blood which had dribbled from his nostrils. 'Twenty,' he mumbled, holding his hand up to his nose. 'I'm really sorry, Jack.'

'Twenty grand's not so bad. Well done, Will. Where's the money.'

Will laid his head back on the floor. 'I haven't got it,' he whimpered.

'Haven't got it?' Kelly asked with mock astonishment. 'What are all those tractors out there, then? Every one of them's worth more than twenty grand apiece.'

'Yeah, but I haven't paid for them. Business was terrible and Susan needed a lot of things when the baby came.'

'I bet she did,' Kelly laughed. 'Even after all the money I gave her when we divorced.' He straightened his legs, leant down and lifted Will up by the collar of his jacket. He half dragged, half led Susan's cringing husband across his office and pushed him down on a desk covered with a mess of papers. The man was openly blubbering now.

'Right,' Kelly said, still holding the man's collar. 'I don't need it right now, as it happens. I can give you a bit of time.'

'Thanks, Jack,' Will whimpered.

'Meet me at the Merton Hotel with it, tomorrow, midday. Cash. All right?'

Will's face drained of blood, turning to a sweaty grey. 'I . . . I c . . . can't,' he yammered.

'You haven't got any choice.' Kelly's mouth twitched up. 'You can do it. You know you can. Ask your dad. Tell him what'll happen to you if you don't. That should do the trick.'

Kelly released his grip, thrusting Will backwards on to the desk as he did so. 'See you tomorrow, then.'

He turned and walked out through the showroom to his Land Rover.

Without looking back, he climbed in, gunned the V8 engine into life and skidded off the forecourt on to the Hereford road. There was a smile on his face. He didn't make a habit of bullying, but the fat, flash bastard had deserved it.

After half a mile, he turned into a narrow lane and headed across country to do the shopping Bowring had asked him to.

9

In a pair of ramshackle barns nestling beneath a wooded hill ten miles north of Hereford, Kelly found what he wanted. On rows of ancient metal racks in Bill Bache's Famous Army Surplus Stores was enough ex-military equipment to kit out a small army with everything except firearms. He could even have bought a couple of armoured personnel carriers and a tank, if he'd wanted. He wandered around happily for an hour until he had gathered up all the boots, belts, bergens, knives, survival kits, OG and DPM clothing Bowring had specified and loaded them into the Land Rover.

Satisfied with his purchases, though uncertain where Bowring expected them to be used, he drove back down the old Roman road towards the sleepy little city. After a few miles, he pulled up outside a black-and-white pub. The soldiers he'd been talking to in Hereford the day before had told him that it had recently been bought by Mick Jones, the son of an Ebbw Vale miner and another ex-member of H Squadron.

'Bloody hell! Jack Kelly!' His one-time comrade-in-arms almost leapt over the bar to greet him. 'How are you?'

Kelly grinned. 'Pretty good, Mick. You?'

'Bored fucking shitless,' the big Welshman said

out of the side of his mouth. 'Here, come into the dining-room – it's empty as usual. What do you want to drink? Want some lunch? Course you do.' He turned as he led Kelly through a low doorway. 'Angie! Bring us two bloody great sirloins.'

He ushered Kelly into a picturesque timber-framed room, full of rustic tables and chairs and chintz curtains. He waved him into a chair. 'Pint of the local?'

Kelly shook his head. 'I'd rather have red wine.'

'Turned into a poof, then, or what?'

Kelly laughed. 'No. Just working abroad, Mick. You lose the taste for bitter.'

'I'll get the best bloody bottle in the house!' The Welshman went out for a few minutes and returned with a venerable claret and two glasses. He pulled out a chair opposite Kelly and lowered his large frame into it.

'So, boyo,' Jones said as he heaved the cork out of the bottle. 'What have you been up to? I haven't heard a thing.'

Kelly shook his head and laughed. 'I'm glad to say I can't tell you.'

'You lucky bastard! Do you know, the biggest challenge I've got running this place is making sure the minibus turns up on the right night to collect the crib team, and the occasional ruck with the brewery about a dodgy barrel of beer. So you've seen a bit of action, then?' he asked enviously.

'Just a bit.'

'Where?'

'I told you, I can't say,' Kelly grinned. 'But the boys in Hereford told me you were still working – proper work, I mean – and your brother-in-law runs the pub.'

Jones gave him a sharp look. 'Did they? Well, they don't know fuck all. I do the odd bit of CPP. Usual, boring gigs,' he said dismissively. 'But you, you're obviously up to something. You look bloody fit. If whoever's paying you needs reinforcements, you let me know.'

'Could you get through another selection?'

Jones looked surprised. 'Not without a bit of training.'

'I doubt there's much chance of anything coming up, but you never know. Anyway, what news of the other lads?'

Kelly and his old friend settled down to a few hours of reminiscing. They had done ten years together, and there was a lot to talk about. From time to time, Jones tried to trick Kelly into giving away something about his current job, but Kelly neatly side-stepped with a laugh. As they talked, Jones took no notice of what was going on in the pub even though, to Kelly's surprise, it became quite busy as lunchtime wore on. But no one disturbed them in the little dining-room.

Kelly drove off a few hours later, leaving the Welshman shaking his head in envy at the sight of all the khaki tack in the back of the Land Rover.

Kelly was welcomed with more reserve in the Sergeants' Mess at Stirling Lines that evening. Despite the close comradeship that existed when you were in the SAS, once you'd left you were an outsider, no longer privy to the Regiment's more covert activities.

Nevertheless, Kelly was a multi-decorated ex-sergeant, part of SAS folklore, and as such deserved a respectful reception. Besides, those men who were reaching the compulsory end of their stretch were anxious to keep tabs on new job opportunities.

Kelly walked back to his hotel, too drunk to risk driving through the town. But he slept soundly enough and woke next day with plenty of time to set off up the steep hill east out of the city for a tough eight-mile run.

He treated himself to a large breakfast when he got back to the Merton Hotel, and sat with a paper, waiting for Will.

Kelly saw Susan walk into the bar and wondered if she had come to plead on her husband's behalf. But if she was feeling nervous or resentful, she wasn't showing it.

Kelly got up from where he had been sitting. 'Hello, Sue. What happened to Will?'

'What do you think happened to him? He was too scared to come. I left him at home crying like a baby,' she said disdainfully.

Kelly nodded his head. 'Do you want a drink?'

'Just coffee.'

Kelly walked over to the bar and ordered it. He came back and sat down opposite his ex-wife. 'Why was he scared? Hasn't he got the money?'

'No. He hasn't. He didn't dare go to his dad. I didn't know it, but he's borrowed a lot from him already over the last few years. In fact, as far as I can see, the whole bloody business is subsidized by the old man.'

'Couldn't he get it anywhere else?'

'No, of course not. He's too much of a prat.'

'What does he think's going to happen, then?'

'He thinks you'll kill him, or at least beat the living crap out of him. I told him you won't, but he doesn't believe me.'

'Do you think I won't?'

'I know you won't; you're not that much of a bastard.'

'Are you so sure?'

She nodded. 'You've never scared me, Jack. What you did used to – when you were away. I used to lie awake all night wondering where you were and if you'd been killed. Every time they reported a killing in Ireland or anywhere, I thought it was you, until they gave a name. I drove the Wives' Support Group mad.'

Kelly didn't say anything. He looked at her, with her deep-brown eyes and the good, strong features of a country girl.

'Anyway,' she went on, 'I've brought the money. My dad just picked it up from the bank. He wasn't too happy, but he said I was going to get it anyway when he died. Mind, he did say Will could do with a good thumping.'

Susan reached into a bag she had brought in with her and pulled out a large brown envelope. 'It's all in fifties. Do you want to count it somewhere? I've got a receipt here for you to sign.'

Kelly looked at the envelope. It seemed absurd that the contents of a small brown paper package should mean so much.

He shook his head. 'No. I don't want to count it.' He looked into Susan's worried eyes. 'I don't want it. I don't need it. You have it. Put it on deposit and keep it for some real problem. You never know, you may find you want to leave Will and it doesn't sound as if he could afford much maintenance.'

Susan looked at him, then down at the envelope, still clasped in her hands.

'But,' she said, against all her instincts, 'I can't . . . It's yours.'

Kelly shrugged. 'It's yours now. I've given it to you. Put it back in your bag and take it straight to the bank when you go.'

There was a look of intense gratitude, and excitement in her eyes. 'But Jack, I want to give you something back.'

Jack shifted in his chair, feeling an erection coming on. She was offering herself to him, there and then – and not just as repayment for a debt. He wanted her, had the opportunity, the time, a room upstairs.

He shook his head and cleared his throat. 'You don't have to give me anything.'

'But I want to, Jack.'

'No way. I didn't come back here to wreck your marriage. What's done's done between us.'

She looked at him bleakly, unwilling to have her offer rejected.

Wordlessly, she put the package back in her bag and stood up, leaving her coffee untouched.

She turned and took a couple of steps, then looked back. 'Thanks, Jack. I'll never forget.'

He watched her neat little bottom, firm in black leggings, leave the bar and he sighed. Hell, he thought, I could have done with it, too.

That evening, when Kelly arrived back at The Hollies with the supplies he had bought, Michelle was alone. He was struck by the great differences, and certain similarities, between her and his former wife. The main difference as far as he was concerned was that Michelle was totally unavailable.

In the previous nights he had stayed in the house

with her, she had treated him as if they were the same sex, or brother and sister. No put-down, no rejection – just complete indifference. Either there was something wrong with her, or she was just too dedicated to her work for Bowring. And though he was fairly sure that there was no sexual relationship between her and the boss, he couldn't restrain a feeling of envy at Bowring's influence over her.

This time, Gallagher wasn't there. Michelle cooked a dinner that would have passed muster at any Côte d'Azur restaurant he'd ever been to, though she did it, Kelly guessed, because she had been told to. As they ate together, she brought him up to date.

During his two days away, a lot of groundwork had been done on the Pope's UK tour. Details of every rally venue and all routes that had already been fixed had been given to them by Monsignor di Montefalco.

Lyke and Dowson had appeared, walking around Summerfold, as if they were weekend guests at a shooting party, Michelle said. With Bowring and Haynes, they had been poring over the maps Terry had made on his computer, approaching the task as if it were SOS who had been ordered to make the hit. Two SOS men who had been employed in El Salvador had arrived, spent three hours with Bowring and left immediately for India. Andy, Michelle said, had been sent to London.

When they had finished eating, Michelle looked at her watch. 'We have to go up to Summerfold now. Major Bowring has a guest from London he wants us to meet.'

Michelle phoned HQ to say they were on their way. Leaving the lights on in The Hollies, and the intruder alarms and a scanning CCTV camera to guard the place, she and Kelly set off up the tunnel. As they went, she pointed out some features of the underground passage that he had missed on his previous trips along it.

At either end of the tunnel, just inside the doors, was a narrow slot in the roof. Retracted in the slots were half-inch steel sheets which could be dropped to block off the way in or out to anyone who didn't happen to have an oxyacetylene lamp and a lot of time on their hands.

Also concealed in the roof, every twenty yards, were small explosive charges primed to release canisters of red phosphorus into the restricted air, a useful substance with the property of absorbing oxygen; in combat it was used in grenades to flush out armoured personnel carriers. Here, the charges were linked and could be activated by a continuous detonation cord.

There was also, Michelle said, a remotely operated choke on the air inlet which he had seen half-way along the tunnel. Similar systems were also installed in the lower tunnel that ran from the well to the ice house. All entrances were monitored by CCTVs.

Even without the overt presence of armed men or guard dogs, Kelly concluded, you could house a US President in Summerfold with reasonable peace of mind. It was, he thought, all a bit over the top, but then he'd already learnt that Bowring worked on the SAS principle of eliminating or diminishing every risk he could.

There was a group gathered in a large drawing-room at the front of the house, on the other side of the hall from the library.

Miss MacFarlane was sitting quietly on one side,

and James was serving drinks, but there was no doubt both were included in Bowring's conference.

Bowring, Haynes, Lyke, Dowson and a fifth man whom Kelly didn't know were sitting on large leather chesterfields in front of an unnecessary log fire.

Despite the brandy glasses and cigars, there was an air of sober alertness to the party. They all rose when Michelle and Kelly walked in.

'Evening, Jack. How did you get on?'

'Got all the gear, boss. Checked out the Sergeants' Mess. I've made notes on some potential recruits.'

'Good. Let Nanny have them in the morning. Did you see your ex-wife?'

'Yes,' Kelly said simply.

Bowring nodded without expression. 'Right. I want you both to meet an old friend of mine, Harry Cotterell, from MI6. He has very kindly agreed to tell us a bit about Sufuf Allah. Harry?'

Everyone sat down again except Cotterell. He was tall, blond and dressed in an impeccable three-piece tweed suit. When he spoke, his voice and every gesture suggested a background of Eton and a regiment Guards regiment, belying his first-class degree in modern history from Oxford.

'A bit, I'm afraid, is all I have to tell you about Sufuf Allah – the Ranks of God. We've only become aware of their existence fairly recently, but what we've heard has worried us. It seems to be composed of the more viciously militant previous members of several other organizations – Hezbollah, Al Fatah, Islamic Jihad, PLFP, Abu Nidal – all committed without reservation to the destruction of Israel, with representatives from half a dozen different Arab nations. In so far as they are administered at all, the administrative base is in

Beirut, though there is certainly a presence in Baghdad. Assad won't have anything to do with them in Syria. We don't know but we guess funding is largely Iraqi and Libyan. We have unconfirmed reports of training camps in the Bekhar valley. Anyway most members would have already received extensive training in their previous organizations. Unlike many of these Islamic groupings, there is no identifiable connection with any European terrorist group; we have, for instance, no evidence of liaison with the Provisional IRA or INLA. So far, we've positively identified five prominent members of Sufuf Allah.'

Cotterell reached behind him and picked up a folder from the table beside the sofa. He pulled out five eight by ten black and white photographs and passed them around to his audience, who studied them as he continued.

'The two known positively to have been actively involved in assassination and sabotage, and the ones to watch, are known as Abdul abu Said and Salah Mahmoud. Of course, it's perfectly possible the others have been too.' He turned to Bowring. 'Until Major Bowring is able to tell me where you expect these people to become active, I can't offer you our most recent monitoring of their movements, such as it is. I am here, as the major has explained to some of you, in an unofficial capacity, and it is only our respect for your organization and some of the operations it has successfully mounted that I'm prepared to tell you what I have. Of course, we fully understand why other governments find it necessary to employ people such as yourselves, and we are pragmatic about your own need for secrecy, but, in the end, we do expect a quid pro quo for any help we might give you.'

Bowring nodded with a smile. It was clear to Kelly that the two men knew and understood each other well.

Later, when Cotterell had completed his briefing with more details of the style and *modus operandi* of the terrorists he had identified, the party broke into smaller groups. Haynes and Kelly excused themselves and headed for the billiard-room.

Over a vicious game of snooker, they discussed Cotterell's presence at their HQ.

'Frankly,' Haynes said, 'it's a bloody miracle that a senior man from MI6 is prepared to come and brief a group of mercenaries.'

'I don't know,' Kelly answered. 'It seems to me that Bowring has spent a lot of effort keeping in with his Establishment mates. I mean, he's one of them after all; and I don't suppose he's ever done anything to embarrass them.'

'You mean he's never let them know if he's done anything that might. But to get right inside the intelligence services like that' – Haynes shook his head – 'it's amazing. Did you recognize any of them mug shots?'

Kelly shook his head. 'No. Abdul abu Said looks like the worst of them. If he's not the boss, he must be very close to him. Not a kisser you'd easily forget.'

'Yeah, well, if you want to stay alive on this job, you don't want to forget any of them.'

Bowring came to The Hollies in the morning.

'I want you to go to London and meet up with Gallagher. He's been watching a flat in South Ken for the last couple of days. He'll tell you what's going on.'

'OK, boss,' Kelly said, hardly excited about the idea of static surveillance.

'Take a set of these shots up,' Bowring said, giving him copies of the photographs Cotterell had produced the evening before. 'We may be able to get a cross-ref on them.'

Michelle took Kelly to Dorking station, since Gallagher had the hire car and there wasn't a spare at HQ. A little over an hour later, he was getting out of a taxi in Queen's Gate. He checked the address Bowring had given him: it was a slightly tatty hotel occupying one of the formerly grand terraced houses. He went in. There was no one at the reception desk so he let himself into a shoebox of a lift, took it to the fifth floor and walked down a poky landing to room fifty-three.

He knocked. There was no immediate reply. After ten seconds, the door flew open in front of him, to reveal a small, scruffy bedroom. 'It's OK, Andy. It's Jack,' he said, keeping dead still.

Gallagher stepped from behind the door, holding his nine-milly in both hands. He lowered the gun when he saw that Kelly was alone. 'Hello, Jack. I didn't expect you so soon. Welcome to my five-star accommodation.'

Kelly followed Gallagher into the room and closed the door. On a dressing-table in front of the window were a full ashtray, several empty Marlboro packets, a newspaper, a pair of binoculars and a Canon camera fitted with a massive 600mm lens.

'How's it going?' Kelly asked.

'It's a bummer,' Gallagher said sourly. 'A bunch of students. I've logged over twenty mugs. Of course, I haven't been at it round the clock.'

'What's the story, then?'

'Hasn't Bowring briefed you?'

'No. He said you would.'

'OK. I'll tell you. The boss sent me to a meet with one of his contacts – an old colleague of yours, as it happens.'

'What? H Squadron?'

'Aye. Though this guy's a bit older than you; a Taffy called Mick Jones.'

Kelly laughed out loud. 'The lying bastard!'

'What?'

'I saw him only yesterday in this pub he's got outside Hereford. He told me he was bored shitless running the place, and he tried like hell to pump me for information. I guess he must keep tabs on a lot of the boys when he's up there. Did you tell him about me?'

'No, course not.'

'Thank Christ for that.'

'Aye, but he'll soon know: we've got a date with him this evening.'

The meeting was in a big, anonymous, Victorian pub in Westminster, full of civil servants on their way home. The Welshman was standing at the bar reading the *Evening Standard* when Gallagher walked in with Kelly behind him. Jones nodded and took a couple of paces towards Gallagher to greet him. Then he saw Kelly and stopped, shaking his head with a rueful grin.

'Hello again, Mick,' Kelly said. 'Has your place got a crib game with this lot tonight?'

Jones laughed. 'I might have guessed you'd be with our old boss. Right, lads. We'll have a quick drink, and then we'll take a walk.'

While they were in the pub, they didn't mention the reason for their meeting, or make any reference to their own current employment. Outside, they got into Gallagher's car – Jones in the front passenger seat, Kelly in the back – and headed back to South Kensington.

Once they were in the car, Jones told Kelly the truth about his current employment.

'I'm sorry about that yesterday. Obviously, the blokes in the Kremlin know what I'm doing; they had to give the references, but apart from a few senior NCOs, none of the others do.' The 'Kremlin' was the SAS's name for the intelligence unit in Hereford. 'I've got a bit of a roving brief, actually, somewhere between the Anti-Terrorist Squad and Special Branch, with a particular interest in the mercenary activities of British nationals.'

'Does Bowring know that?' Gallagher asked.

'Of course he does. And he gives us a lot in return. He's told me that he's interested in a particular bunch of Arab loonies. We've said we'd keep our eyes open. Did you get anything much today?' he asked Gallagher.

'No. This Imam Hafiz Jadid you put me on to is more of a sort of religious guru than a terrorist.'

'What makes you think that?'

'The type of people coming to see him, the people he's been out with. None of them look like soldiers – more like serious students. You get to know what to look for.'

'You're right; he's a sort of holy man, but that doesn't mean he's not dangerous. We think he might be here on a recruitment drive.'

'Why don't you watch him yourself, then?'

Jones laughed. 'Have you any idea how much a stake-out costs us? We have to be bloody sure it's

176

worth it to justify it. You know how tight-fisted all the departments are these days. But Bowring's prepared to do it, and we think there's a connection between this bloke and the Sufuf Allah he's so interested in. The fact of the matter is that there's more and more aggressive militancy developing among a lot of the Muslim students in this country, and a lot of them are very well educated and likely to achieve positions of influence, if not actual power, here.'

Gallagher, driving, shook his head. 'There's no one interesting going to turn up at that place.'

'I'd give it a while longer. Anyway, until your boss tells you to quit.'

'Aye,' Gallagher said, resigned. 'Anyway, Bowring's sent up some mug shots for you; five suspected members of Sufuf Allah. Show him, Jack.'

'We've got six, actually,' Kelly said. 'There's mine from Amman too.' He took the photographs out of an envelope and passed them forward to the Welshman.

'Are these for me?'

'Yes,' Gallagher said. 'But the deal is, you tell us first if any come in.'

'We can't guarantee that. Are you expecting them in?'

The Scot shook his head vaguely. 'Not particularly. But there are always reasons why they might be over here. Of course, we've got people in France and Switzerland looking out for them.'

'Right. You can drop me here,' said Jones. 'I've got a meet in Sloane Square. Let me know what comes up in Queen's Gate, and don't forget, I'll want a set of your shots from there, too.' He turned back towards Kelly. 'I don't suppose I have to tell you, but keep your bloody trap shut about me, or Bowring'll sling you.'

Kelly laughed. 'You didn't get much out of me at lunch yesterday, and that was after two bottles of your best plonk.'

'Plonk? Château-Lafite '75. Fifty quid a bottle, that's worth.' Gallagher stopped the car and Jones let himself out. 'Cheerio, lads. Keep in touch.' Seconds later he was swallowed up in the crowd heading for Sloane Square tube station.

Kelly spent another two days in Queen's Gate taking turns at surveillance with Gallagher. They'd booked a second room in the hotel so that they could get a decent bit of sleep.

At half-past three on the second afternoon, to alleviate his boredom, Kelly decided that he'd tail the first interesting-looking individual to leave the flat opposite.

As Gallagher had told Jones, most of the visitors to Imam Hafiz Jadid looked like earnest, book-loving students. But there was one, apparently a European, who displayed much more assertiveness as he descended the stairs and bumped into another man, who was minding his own business as he entered the five-storey building.

'Right,' Kelly said to his colleague, who'd just returned. 'I'll take my four hours off tailing that character.'

'What the hell for?'

'Something to do. And he looks a lot dodgier than any of our man's other visitors.'

'He hasn't had many whites, that's true. Are you sure he went to see the Imam?'

'I've got a snap of him, through the window of the bloody flat.'

'Good enough. You'd better go or you'll lose him before you've started. Have fun.'

Kelly didn't wait for the ancient lift. He ran down the stairs three at a time and came out of the door of the hotel just in time to see his quarry turning left into Old Brompton Road.

The man was in his mid-twenties, about five feet ten, with short brown hair. He was wearing jeans and a white drill jacket. There was a sort of thrusting arrogance about him as he strode along the busy pavement. Kelly could not have said precisely why he had decided to follow this particular man, beyond the fact that he looked like someone who enjoyed causing mayhem.

It was a slender reason for going to the trouble of tailing the man, and an hour later, Kelly was wondering why he had bothered. Via the Circle and Northern lines, the man led him to a building in Hampstead – a student hostel by the look of it and the people coming and going.

From a distance, Kelly watched the place for a few minutes and came to the conclusion that his quarry, having gone home, would probably stay there. He retraced his route to South Kensington, telling himself that he'd only undertaken the chase to kill a few hours. In any case, it was gratifying to know that his solo surveillance skills weren't too rusty. Street-wise as he undoubtedly was, the guy hadn't suspected a thing.

When Kelly reached the hotel, Gallagher was more cheerful than he had been earlier.

'The boss has been on. He wants us back at HQ, thank God.'

They were back at The Hollies by seven that

evening and were immediately summoned up to Summerfold.

The Pope was due to arrive in England in eight days' time. There was a palpable increase in controlled tension within the English headquarters of SOS; fewer jokes, less lavish hospitality.

Although Bowring was confident that the attempt on His Holiness's life would not be made in India, there was always the possibility, and he had only two men out there to handle it. It was, on his part, a calculated risk. He was ninety-five per cent sure the attempt would take place in Britain, and he wanted his best men on the ground there.

There had been a further complication. As soon as Kelly and Gallagher walked into the library, where James had directed them, Bowring got up from his desk holding a newspaper.

'The *Telegraph*'s man in Paris has picked up a rumour that there was a European mercenary unit involved in the fracas at Fontainebleau. That's going to get them very excited in Whitehall, especially as they know we're interested in Islamic groups at the moment. Frankly, I'd expected to hear from them by now.'

'Boss, why did you tell them what we were after?' Kelly asked.

'If I didn't tell them something, they'd go to a lot more trouble to find out for themselves. This way I at least control what they know; and of course, they give me something back.'

'But the photos we gave Mick Jones yesterday were given to us by MI6.'

'That's simple exploitation of interdepartmental

secrecy and rivalry. I've made it my business to keep contacts with most of them.' Bowring's top lip twitched. 'Sometimes I think they trust me more than each other. As far as France was concerned, it must have been the domestic staff at the house who told French security that they were tied up by Europeans, but there's no way any of us would be identifiable, and they haven't even specified that they're talking about Brits. Anyway, there's bugger all we can do about it now.' He sighed. 'We should have killed them.'

'That's what I thought at the time,' Gallagher said.

Kelly didn't say anything.

'Right,' Bowring went on, with a change of tone. 'Let's have a look at what you got in South Ken.'

Gallagher had brought with him a stack of shots that he and Kelly had taken over the last few days. Bowring took the prints and spread them out on the table in front of him. He inspected each one carefully. When he'd been through them twice, he asked: 'Did you follow up any of these?'

'Only that one,' Kelly said, pointing to the three shots he had taken of the one caucasion visitor to the Imam Hafiz Jadid. 'I tailed him this afternoon to Hampstead, to a hostel mostly used by LSE students. I left him there.'

'None of the others?'

'None of them looked any worse than the rest,' Gallagher said, shrugging. 'Frankly, boss, it was a bit of a waste of time.'

'We'll see. There's a growing amount of militant fundamentalism among Muslim students in this country. If I were planning a hit, I think I'd see if I could make use of them. After all, they know their way around, speak the language properly and I have no doubt there are a few who'd like to get close to the more extreme Islamic groups. In the meantime, we've identified a number of choice hit sites.' Bowring cleared the photographs from the table and laid several maps on it. The first was of the whole of England and Wales.

'If I were running Sufuf Allah, I'd choose either here,' he said, putting his finger on Cardiff, 'the rally in the Arms Park, or here, at Aintree Racecourse, where they're holding an open-air mass, or here' – he pointed at the heart of London – 'at the final rally in Hyde Park. Terry and Michelle are checking them out now, making a full photographic survey. Michelle is interviewing officials and should be able to establish the Pope's planned movements at each venue. I want you two to carry on checking on local Islamic groups. Jack, take Manchester and Cardiff. Andy, you follow up more of Jadid's visitors, or see where he goes to talk to any groups. What we're looking for is any connection with the six faces we already have.'

Kelly hired a Ford Sierra and drove straight to South Wales, where he spent a day trawling around the areas of Swansea and Cardiff where most of the Bangladeshi, Somali and Yemeni populations lived. He also looked at the mosques and other public Muslim buildings. Back in his hotel that evening, he rang Bowring.

'Hello, boss. I'd have to be here a month to get anything useful. I need some short cuts.'

'Leave it with me,' Bowring said, and rang off.

Kelly had swum forty lengths of the hotel's empty

pool by seven-fifteen next morning. As he climbed out and began to dry himself, a man appeared through the swing doors from the hotel and sauntered across the tiled floor.

'Mr Kelly?'

He was about thirty, prematurely balding, and dressed in a baggy linen suit, with a silk shirt open at the collar.

'Who are you?' Kelly asked.

'Mick Jones sent me,' the man answered with a broad Cardiff accent. 'Said you needed a hand.'

Kelly nodded. 'Great. I'll meet you outside in ten minutes.'

'Mine's the green Daihatsu.'

In the Japanese 4WD vehicle, the driver introduced himself. 'Barry Bevan. Freelance. Used to be in CID here. Didn't like the discipline – or the money. The residents think I deal drugs so they try not to take too much notice of me. Inspector Jones tells me you need to identify a few of the Muslim groups here. I can tell you the name of any of them who are anyone in South Wales. What exactly are you looking for?'

Kelly told him – without saying why – and pulled on a baseball cap and dark glasses while Bevan drove him around, pointing out houses and individuals from his all too conspicuous car.

As they drove, stopped, looked and waited, Kelly pressed Bevan for information on possible student groups, but the Welshman didn't have much to offer. At the end of the day, having told Bevan he'd contact him if he needed him again, and feeling frustrated, Kelly contacted Bowring.

'Look, boss, there don't seem to be any organizations of the type we're looking for. The man you got Mick to put on to me knew his stuff; he's been hanging around the ghettos for years and he had no real leads.'

'OK. Drop it. Get up to Manchester. Book into the Piccadilly. I'll have someone round to you first thing in the morning.'

'Right. How's Andy doing?'

'Getting somewhere. I may need you back in a hurry, so check in every hour.'

It was several years since Kelly had been to Manchester. As far as he could see, the most significant changes to have taken place, besides the general cleaning up of the city, were the new trams and the increase in the number of beggars and prostitutes on the streets. He didn't doubt, though, that the long-established Islamic presence in the city was as strong as ever.

It was an Indian with the accent of a native Mancunian who turned up to see him at his hotel next morning. Ahmed Qureshi's family were originally from the Punjab, but his grandfather had brought his family to England in the early thirties to found what was now a substantial textile trading company. Ahmed, in his mid-twenties, had been at Manchester Grammar School and was now a journalist on one of the big local dailies. Utterly irreligious himself, he had nevertheless found himself covering a lot of news concerning the city's diverse Muslim community.

Outside, in Kelly's car, Kelly told Qureshi what they were looking for.

'Fundamentalist Islamic student groups? Plenty of scope there. I don't know what the hell they think they're going to achieve; chance to sit around and shout at each other, I shouldn't wonder. There's a very active bunch of them in one of the University halls of residence. Let's take a look at that first.'

Qureshi directed him south towards the University, along Oxford Road. They turned right by a municipal park and pulled up just short of a large, ugly, sixties building.

'I doubt if there's much going on now, but I'll pop in and check.'

Qureshi leapt out of the car and strode purposefully into the students' accommodation.

Kelly waited twenty minutes, using the time to scrutinize the men and women going in and out of the building. Glancing in his mirror as he had done regularly while he'd been waiting, he received an abrupt shock. Walking towards the rear of his car, with three young Asian students, was the man he had followed from Imam Hafiz Jadid's flat in Queen's Gate to the hostel in Hampstead.

Instinctively, Kelly sank down in his seat and pulled the peak of his baseball cap lower over his face, even though he knew he hadn't been spotted by his quarry in London. His pulse quickened and his nerve ends tingled. The group were passing his car now. He heard the white student talking, with a sharp London accent – '. . . we'll have to finalize it tonight, though . . .' – and carry on out of Kelly's hearing.

With a jolt, he saw Qureshi emerge from the student building and walk towards the car. He prayed that the journalist wouldn't say anything until he'd got back in.

The others, walking towards Qureshi, took no

notice, and he let himself into the passenger side before he said anything.

Kelly didn't start the car at once. He held up his hand for a moment as he watched the Englishman and the three Asians disappear through the door by which Qureshi had just left. Once they were in, Kelly started the car and drove on past the entrance.

'I knew one of those,' he said with excitement. 'I've seen him in London – the English one – visiting some kind of militant iman.'

'There are quite a number of white Muslims up here,' Qureshi said. 'Funny lot, but they're very committed.'

'Did you find out anything?'

'Yes, I did. There's some kind of meeting tonight, of the Council of Muslim Students. I was trying to see if I could muscle my way into it, but I think it'd be tricky – them not knowing me. They didn't suspect anything, though; it's lucky my dad always made me keep up my Urdu. I just said I was interested in getting involved, but they said I'd have to come to the next open meeting.'

'Still, you could hang around, couldn't you?'

'Of course I can. And I'll be able to tell you if that white bloke's part of it.'

Kelly was surprised but relieved that what he had thought was going to be a wild-goose chase had yielded a hard connection. He couldn't keep the elation from his voice when he rang Bowring.

'I've met up with my chum from Hampstead,' he said. 'He's up here to discuss something with a group of Muslim students.'

'Good. Can you leave the fellow who's with you to keep an eye on him?'

'I'd rather stay up here.'

'I need you in London, Jack. Can this other chap cope?'

'Well, probably. He's quite on the ball.'

'Fix it, and make sure he keeps in contact. Then get back to South Ken and contact me as soon as you're there.'

'OK, boss.'

Kelly spent an hour briefing Qureshi, without giving him much of an idea of what might be going to happen. The journalist was aware that he was involved in something bigger than mere news gathering. It didn't take much to convince him of the need for discretion, particularly since, as Kelly told him, there'd be a much bigger story in the end.

10

Kelly turned wearily into Queen's Gate from busy Cromwell Road and parked on a double yellow line a short distance from the hotel where he and Gallagher had stayed. Bowring had told him to get there and await instructions. Kelly cursed the lack of a telephone in the hired car and hoped he wouldn't have to wait long.

He didn't. Within a minute of his turning off the engine, he saw Jim Mason walking up the tree-lined street towards him.

Kelly wound down the front passenger window. 'What's the story?'

The butler poked his head into the Sierra and said: 'Major Bowring's in his car, a grey Daimler round the corner. You're to go and see him. I'll stay here with this one.'

Kelly climbed out and left the driver's door open.

He found Bowring parked in the adjacent street and opened the back door.

'Get in, Jack.'

Kelly slid in beside Bowring. The interior of the Daimler smelt of cigar smoke and leather.

'We've had a bit of luck. Your Palestinian's shown up,' Bowring said curtly. 'Andy was on to Jadid. Followed him to a house in a mews at the end of this road. Then he came out after an hour or so, with the chap you photographed in Amman.' He grinned and went on. 'I'm glad we've had a result. Andy's whinging was getting tiresome and I was beginning to think Jones had given us a bum steer. And now you've picked up this English Muslim in Manchester. I think we're getting somewhere. Just in time, too. I imagine my friends in Whitehall have worked out what's going on, so we'll have to tread rather carefully. Our contract with the Vatican is unequivocal on the question of not alerting the authorities here.'

'But they'll be on to it PDQ.'

'Not quick enough. We're a lot further on than they are. But it means you'll have to tell Jones you've drawn a blank. He'll forgive us when it's all over – I hope.' Bowring shook his head. 'That's the trouble with working on one's own doorstep.'

A radio on the seat beside Bowring wheezed into life.

'Blackbird?' Kelly recognized Gallagher's voice. 'Coaltit here. Are you receiving me? Over.'

Bowring picked up the radio. 'This is Blackbird. Carry on, Coaltit.'

'I'm at 57K142.'

Bowring opened a London A-Z and flipped through it until he found a page covering an area half a mile west of them.

'Go on, Coaltit.'

'I have Polecat in view. He's talking to a Joshua Reynolds in the street outside the tube station. Which shall I take?'

'Stick with Polecat. Keep in contact. I'm sending Wagtail to join you. Over and out.'

Bowring turned to Kelly. 'You're Wagtail.'

'You don't say. Who's Joshua Reynolds?'

'One of the five mug shots Cotterell gave us.'

'Shit. They're coming in fast.'

'But complacent, if they're chattering in the street. We can only take one, so we'll stay with Polecat for now. He's likely to be a general-purpose gofer and getting around more than the high-ups.'

Bowring picked up a dark-blue tourist's rucksack from the floor of the car. 'Here's a radio, an A-Z and a nine-milly in the wash-bag. To give your position, reverse the page number and add a digit to the grid. They're in Earls Court Road now. If Polecat takes the tube, you won't get anything from Andy until they come up for air. Once you've caught up with him, try and keep them in vision. I'll be cruising nearby. If you need back-up, I'll come in.'

'OK. You just want him tailed – no contact?'

'Yes. We don't want to touch them until we know which of them is doing the shooting, and preferably from where. I thought that balls-up in France might put them off the whole plan, but they're obviously anxious to make their mark as soon as possible. Besides they won't get a crack at His Holiness like this for some time. Now, just brief me on what you saw in Manchester.'

Kelly gave him a more detailed description of the Englishman he had seen go into the hall of residence with the three Asians, and told him what Qureshi had said about the meeting that was due to take place there that evening.

'This Qureshi should be OK,' Bowring said when Kelly had finished. 'He doesn't know it, but he's worked for me a couple of times before. His editor's an old friend of mine; he was the son of the gardener at Summerfold. Bright man. Got a scholarship to Manchester University from Guildford Grammar School.'

Kelly couldn't help a smile at the diversity of Bowring's contacts.

'Jack, most people like to be used, provided you tell them that's what you're doing, and reward them, of course. Tell James to get back here, will you.'

Kelly nodded, took the rucksack and let himself out of the car.

Back in the Sierra, Kelly took the radio from the bag and opened the channel. He also unpacked the Browning – fitted with a silencer – pushed thirteen rounds into the magazine and stuffed it into a pocket of his leather jacket.

In the absence of any communication from Gallagher, he started the car, pulled on his baseball cap and sunglasses and drove unhurriedly towards the mews where Bowring had said that Gallagher had followed Polecat.

On the way, he stopped to buy an *Evening Standard* from a newsvendor. He pulled into a gap opposite the eastern exit of the double-ended mews which gave him a clear view down it. He turned the motor off, lit a cigarette and opened his paper like any bored minicab driver.

The radio buzzed. 'Blackbird. This is Coaltit, are you receiving me? Over.'

Kelly picked it up.

'This is Wagtail. Where are you?'

'Polecat's turning back into the mews.'

Kelly glanced down the mews. Seconds later, he saw a sallow man of medium height walk into the cobbled street from the other end – too far for Kelly to positively recognize him as the man who had tailed Bowring in Amman.

He started his car and drove leisurely into the mews. He glanced at the front doors of the small houses, as if searching for a number. The man walking towards him looked briefly at him without breaking his step. Kelly drew level with him, and with a rush of adrenalin, saw that Gallagher hadn't been mistaken. The Palestinian was even wearing the same clothes as in the shots Kelly had taken outside the Hotel Philadelphia.

Kelly drove slowly by; Polecat ignored him. He carried on until he passed under a white-stucco archway at the end of the mews. Gallagher was waiting on the far side of it, out of Polecat's sight. Kelly made no sign of recognition. He pulled up fifty yards away, put on a tiny throat mike and a headset and put the radio in his pocket.

He opened his *Evening Standard* again.

'Coaltit?'

'I've got you.'

'What's the score?'

'Polecat's back in his den. We sit.'

'I'll go back and take the other end.'

Kelly started the Sierra again and took the next road on the right which backed on to the mews. He ended up where he had been parked before Polecat came back. This time he got out of the car and walked a few yards out of sight of the narrow lane.

He had smoked three more cigarettes when a black taxi turned in and rattled over the cobbles. As Kelly strolled back towards his car he saw the cab stop halfway down the mews. He got back into his car and his radio fizzed into life.

'Wagtail?'

'Receiving.'

'He's taken a cab, my way.'

'OK. I'm on to him. You take one too. I'll tell you where.'

Kelly turned into the mews as the taxi drove through the archway, indicating right. He reached the other end in time to see it heading up towards Cromwell Road. There was only one other car between them.

He had no trouble sticking with them, trusting that the anonymous beige Sierra wouldn't arouse Polecat's guard if he looked back. He followed the taxi through the thickening early-evening traffic as it crossed the main radial routes of Cromwell Road and Kensington High Street, heading north.

Gallagher came on the air.

'I've got a cab stopping. Where to?'

'Head towards Notting Hill Gate. I'll give you a number in a moment.'

Polecat's cab turned east on to Bayswater Road. Kelly grabbed the A-Z and opened it on his steering wheel, ready to give Gallagher a reference as soon as he could. Meanwhile his quarry carried on along the broad thoroughfare for half a mile, before diving abruptly to the left into a maze of white-stucco streets, where every other building was an hotel or guest-house catering mainly for Middle Eastern visitors.

The taxi stopped in a narrow, leafy square and Polecat got straight out and walked across the pavement, up the steps of one of the hotels.

Kelly drove past and round to the far side of the square, where he still had a view of the hotel entrance. He switched off his engine and flipped through the pages of the A-Z as he got through to Gallagher.

'Coaltit?'

'Hello, Wagtail,' the Scot said huskily from the back of his taxi.

'95K476. Polecat's gone to ground. Arrive here on foot and raise me. Over.'

'OK. Over and out.'

For the third time, Kelly picked up his newspaper, of which he had so far read no more than the front-page headlines, and kept his eyes on the hotel. There was nothing in particular about it to help him; it was like thousands of others in the area – just the sort of place to house an Arab associate of Polecat's. Kelly wondered which particular associate; perhaps another of Cotterell's mug shots.

'Wagtail?'

'Receiving you, Coaltit.'

'I'm on foot, walking into the south side of the square.'

'Clock my car. Our man's dead opposite.'

Gallagher sauntered into Kelly's view and strolled down the far side of the square, slowing his pace almost imperceptibly as he passed the hotel. He carried on, crossed over into the square's gardens and sat on a bench beneath the canopy of a large plane tree. He pulled his A-Z from his pocket and began to study it.

An hour dragged by. Groups of Arabs in djellabas and their womenfolk in yashmaks arrived back at the hotels, on foot and in taxis, with great bags of shopping. A younger generation in leather blousons and jeans came out, on their way to hang around the shopping malls in Queensway.

Gallagher and Kelly kept silent; they had no need to communicate until, at last, Polecat reappeared. He came out of his hotel and turned north, seemingly unaware of Gallagher sitting under his tree. Kelly started the Sierra and drove round the square in time to see Gallagher turn left into a road at the far end.

Kelly glanced down the road as he drove past. Apart from Gallagher, he saw no one. There were cars and vans parked tightly along both sides of the narrow road, and a 'No Entry' sign. Kelly could see that the other end gave on to a busy shopping street. He drove on and took the next left, running parallel to Gallagher's turning. He accelerated up to the busy street, then nosed left into the traffic and left again, towards Gallagher.

He had gone fifty yards when he saw Polecat, twenty yards ahead, leaning motionless against the back of a van, with a hand in the bulging pocket of his bomber jacket.

Kelly's guts tightened. Gallagher was strolling along the pavement towards the van, quite unaware of what was waiting for him behind it. Kelly glanced in his mirror. No other vehicle had followed him into the road. He dropped his speed to a crawl, winding his window down, as if he were looking for somewhere to park. Ten yards from the Palestinian, he pulled the Browning from his pocket.

At the same time, Polecat had discreetly pulled something from his jacket. He glanced down the otherwise empty road at Kelly, angrily impatient for him to drive past. When Kelly stopped fifteen feet from him, Polecat's eyes flashed wild with suspicion and indecision.

Calmly, without haste, Kelly lifted the Browning.

A double-tap, two muffled shots, straight to the head. There was just time to see a look of amazed disbelief on the man's face before he crumpled to the ground.

Before the Palestinian's body had completely come to rest on the oily grit of the road surface, the Sierra was in gear and roaring up the road, and Gallagher had reached the van.

'Coaltit. Walk on. Polecat's retired.'

'What the fuck happened?' Gallagher's voice was thick with shock.

'Just walk on past. Leave it,' Kelly said, trying to convey urgency without giving away to any airwave eavesdroppers the momentousness of the balls-up he and his colleague had just caused.

Gallagher's step faltered as he glanced down at the motionless body between the back of the van and a battered old Jaguar. 'OK, Wagtail,' he said, swivelling his eyes to look fifty yards straight ahead where a trio of young Arabs had turned into the road, walking towards him.

He carried on at a casual walk, burning up inside at the incompetence he had displayed in getting sussed so easily. He passed the Arab boys, reached the busy main road at the end and crossed straight over into a vast shopping mall that had been created from one of London's grand old department stores to cater for the unending stream of visitors to that part of London.

He walked briskly through the browsing crowds and out the other side, then turned up a quiet street leading to Bayswater Road.

'Wagtail? Are you receiving?'

'This is Blackbird,' Bowring's voice came back to him. 'Go ahead, Coaltit.'

'I'm clear.'

'Double check. I'll pick you up at 95K571, westward in twenty minutes. Wagtail, take that car back to the hire company immediately.'

'Roger, Blackbird,' Kelly's Liverpudlian drawl sounded unruffled.

Gallagher checked his A-Z, zigzagging through a maze of small roads towards Notting Hill Gate, where he dived down into the tube station, bought a ticket and switchbacked through the system of escalators and tunnels before emerging on the south side of the road to walk east back up Bayswater Road. Even if Polecat's people had put a team of watchers on him, which he very much doubted, he would have stretched them too far by now.

He spotted Bowring's Daimler cruising towards him as he reached his RV point. The car slowed and the rear door was opening before it came to a stop. Gallagher was in and the car moving off in less than three seconds.

'What happened?' Bowring asked tersely.

'Dunno, boss. He must have sussed me.'

'That was bloody careless of you,' Bowring hissed through tight lips. 'I've given the police an anonymous tip-off. With luck they'll have Polecat out of the way before his friends find out what's happened to him. With luck. Then we'll just have to keep our fingers crossed that no one took the number of Jack's car. If it gets traced back to us, it's not going to be easy to explain things to our Whitehall friends.'

'Aye, well, I'm sorry, boss. I was certain he wasn't on to us.'

'It may not be the end of the world. In fact, if his friends simply lose him, that could help; it's only if they know it was us who hit him that we'll have problems.'

Bowring arranged to pick up Kelly outside Gloucester Road tube station.

'Did you have to kill him?' Bowring asked as soon as he was in the car.

'Yes, I did. He was on to Andy. He'd have taken him out and gone back with the information that they'd been sussed and we'd have lost the lot of them.'

'And they'd have cancelled their operation, which is what we're being paid for.'

'And I couldn't let him kill Andy, could I?'

Bowring nodded. 'It's OK. It'll be much more satisfying to take them in the act.'

Satisfaction, that's what you're in it for, Kelly thought.

'Right,' Bowring went on. 'We'll go for a walk in Hyde Park. James, drop us by the Queen Mother's Gate.'

There was the usual summer crowd milling around the south-eastern corner of the Park. Bowring and his two soldiers strolled unobtrusively among them.

'The Pope's final rally is being held here. His motorcade will leave Westminster Cathedral, go round in front of Buck House and up Constitution Hill to give the punters a good look. They're opening the gates under the Quadrica Arch at Hyde Park Corner. He'll come through that, in front of Apsley House then turn up Park Lane. They'll go the full length of Park Lane and turn into the park at Cumberland Gate. The platform is being erected up there at the top end.' He waved up towards Speakers' Corner and looked at his two mercenaries. 'If they haven't had a crack at him in Cardiff or Aintree, where would you think they'd try and hit him here?' he asked, as if he were setting them a casual brain-teaser.

They stopped. Kelly swept his eyes along the route, that part of it which they could see, from the back of Apsley House to Marble Arch.

'Shit, there's about a dozen useful spots. But anyway, they could just do it from the crowd.'

'Unlikely, no exit,' Bowring said shortly.

'That wouldn't matter to a *hara-kiri* fanatic. They'd think they were going straight to heaven.'

'They wouldn't get near enough,' Gallagher said. 'Even if the DP Squad haven't sussed by then that somebody's going to try and pull something, they'll have hundreds of men on the ground. They'd be mad if they thought they could hit him out there. No, I reckon it'd have to be from one of the buildings along the other side of Park Lane, and they'd try and take him as he goes past.'

'In an armour-plated vehicle?' Bowring said.

'You could pierce the Pope-mobile with a 7.62 round.'

'No guarantee.' Bowring shook his head. 'They'd need something a lot heavier.'

'OK,' Kelly ventured. 'They could set up in any of those hotels – Inn on the Park, Lanesborough, Intercontinental, Londonderry House, The Hilton, Dorchester, Grosvenor House. Bloody hell, that gives them a choice of a few hundred rooms.'

Bowring nodded. 'Correct. We've got rooms booked in most of them for two nights before. Not the Hilton, Londonderry House or the Inn on the Park. I wouldn't choose any of them – too restricted an arc of fire. If no hit's been made by then, I'll have a fifteen-post surveillance team in operation, starting the Tuesday before. Right now, our job is to latch back on to those faces we've got. That gives us the flat in Queen's Gate, the mews house in Earls Court and the hotel in Bayswater. I'll get Michelle and Terry back to support you. Andy, you take Terry; Jack, you can have Michelle . . . and don't look so bloody pleased about it – you know the standing orders.'

The next morning, Michelle joined Kelly in the scruffy hotel opposite Imam Jadid's flat in Queen's Gate. They were watching from a room one floor higher than the previous OP. There wasn't a sign of life in the flat.

'I'll go and make some enquiries,' Michelle said.

In spite of Kelly's arguments, she left and he watched her cross the road and disappear into the building.

Two minutes later, she came out and back to their room.

'He's gone,' she announced. 'I told the caretaker I'd just started teaching at the Lycée in Old Brompton Road and needed a flat in a hurry. He said one had just come vacant – a Lebanese man had taken it for two weeks, but left last night in a hurry with a week paid for. It looks as though you have scared them away.'

A similar story came back from Gallagher at the mews house. The hotel in Bayswater didn't seem worth watching but Kelly and Michelle were able to book themselves into a guest-house opposite after dark that evening and watched it continuously for two days. By now they knew every wrinkle and characteristic of the five 'Joshua Reynolds'. None of them, nor anyone else who particularly excited suspicion, came or went.

Despite their physical proximity and their shared sense of purpose now that they were really on the scent of Sufuf Allah, Michelle maintained the polite, invisible barrier she had erected between them.

Kelly was philosophical; even if she had shown that she was interested in reciprocating his urges, they had a job to do which needed one of them permanently at the window with binoculars and a camera. He adopted a new tactic, and restricted his conversation purely to their immediate task.

'Why are you so quiet?' she asked at the end of the first day. 'Did it upset you to kill that man?'

Kelly shook his head without looking up from the newspaper he was reading.

'So it means nothing that you took his life?' she persisted.

This time Kelly looked up. 'You've never killed anyone, have you?'

'No,' she answered neutrally. 'Not with a direct shot.'

'When you're dealing with a target, you get used to the idea that it's not a person, just a problem to be dealt with. If you worried about upsetting their mums, you'd never be able to do it. I was brought up to think that it was a sin to kill; and so it is, if you know the person or they're not an enemy in a particular conflict. Anyway, this guy was planning to kill the Pope, so they couldn't hold it against me that much – in fact I suppose it's worth a few heavenly brownie points.'

'Did . . . did he die fast?'

Kelly snapped his thumb and forefinger. 'Like that.

Two shots, one hole. The only thing that worried me was I was using high-powered rounds. That's why I had to go for a head shot, otherwise the bullets might have passed right through his thorax and the van behind him where Andy was walking.' He shrugged. 'You have to think of these things as well as everything else, all in a second or two.'

Michelle turned back to the window. 'They say you were quite a hero in the SAS.'

'Do they?' Kelly said unenthusiastically.

'Well, you must have been, to win your Military Medal.'

Kelly laughed. 'That didn't seem very heroic at the time. I got it mainly for getting bloody wet and not leaving my post.'

'But you must have done something more than that.'

Kelly sighed. 'I was the leader of a four-man patrol, dug into a soggy pit above Port Stanley. They dropped us in Sea Kings from *Hermes* with a week's rations, early in May. You should have seen the way the mist rolled off the sea in the mornings. Anyway, we were there nearly four weeks. We sent in Harriers on half a dozen raids to wipe out Argy Chinooks and Pucaras and we sent back a lot of useful stuff on the state of the enemy troops we could see. Even then I could tell the Argies weren't keen to fight. They looked more miserable than we did, and we couldn't even cook ourselves a decent meal for over a fortnight in case they spotted us. It wasn't much of a laugh, and I was bloody pleased to get back, but the brass were chuffed.'

'Was that all?'

'It was enough, but we also took out an enemy

patrol — ten of them, four of us. We had to; at that stage the Argies didn't even know we were on the islands and it would have blown the whole oppo, and we couldn't take them prisoner — we didn't have any food.'

'And you worked in Ireland?'

'Yeah, but I'll tell you about that another time, all right? I'm just trying to crack this crossword.' He nodded at *The Times* on his knee.

Bowring gave Michelle and Kelly two days in Bayswater before he agreed with them that any Sufuf Allah there must have moved out at the same time as the others.

'I wish to God Andy had been more careful, Jack,' he said to Kelly in private back at Summerfold. 'When this job's over, you'll have to give him some refresher training.'

'I don't know if he'd take it from me,' Kelly said.

'He will if I tell him to. In the meantime, all our hot leads in London have gone cold and I'm having trouble getting anything else out of Harry Cotterell and Mick Jones. And I can't tell them any more now — not without revealing our involvement in Polecat's death, which would be tricky. Incidentally, I don't think anyone's reported your car to the police or we'd have heard by now.'

'I don't reckon anyone saw it, unless they happened to be looking out of a window at the time. The gun was silenced, and he went down without any fuss between a van and a car.'

'I'm glad you haven't lost your touch, anyway. In the circumstances it was the only option. The trouble is, all we've got to go on now is your white Muslim in Manchester. He's the only connection with the imam, and that doesn't necessarily mean he's with Sufuf Allah. Qureshi's been in touch, but I'm afraid he doesn't seem to have got much yet, so you and Michelle are going to Manchester in the morning. I'll see what I can do to revive the leads in London.'

Next morning, at the wheel of yet another mundane saloon, this time a Vauxhall Astra, Kelly wished he'd brought his own Range Rover across from France. Not that he'd had an opportunity, and anyway it would only have been more conspicuous. But he did have Michelle for company. It occurred to him how much he would have liked to have stopped and had a long, leisurely lunch with her in some country restaurant, but they didn't have time, and it probably wouldn't have got him anywhere with her. On the whole, they restricted their conversation to the job in hand, and some guarded revelations on her part about Bowring and SOS.

'What made you want to join?' he asked.

'It was a good opportunity for me,' she said. 'There are no other ways I could have done what I'm doing now, not in any official force.'

'They've got a few women attached to the Regiment now,' Kelly said. 'Mind you, I don't think they get to do much killing, mostly surveillance. I suppose that's where Bowring got the idea. Is that what you wanted to do?'

She didn't answer, but Kelly had no doubt at all that she had the strength to go through with anything that Bowring was ever likely to ask of her. And there were certainly advantages in having a resourceful woman on the team; she could make approaches which would be much more difficult for a man without raising suspicions. The only trouble was, she was too pretty for most people not to notice her, and that was a disadvantage. But he didn't press her on her reasons for coming to work for Bowring.

In Manchester, they booked into separate rooms in the Piccadilly. Ahmed Qureshi, bursting with excitement, arrived soon afterwards.

Bowring and Dowson were in the library at Summerfold House, reviewing Operation Parson's Nose.

'It's not going well, Piers. Sooner or later someone's going to draw a connection between us and that balls-up in Fontainebleau.'

'Relax. The French are much more pragmatic than our people about that sort of thing. The only French nationals involved were a handful of Algerian hoodlums from Marseilles; nobody's going to lose much sleep over them. It would suit the security services in Paris much better to treat the whole thing as an inter-Arab dispute of some sort. Certainly if they had conveyed any suspicions of a British involvement to Whitehall, I'd have heard by now.'

'You may be right, but gunning down that Palestinian in a London street in broad daylight, for God's sake!'

'It was the only option. Thank God Kelly still knows how to think on his feet – and how to shoot straight.' He walked over to the window, where the view of the South Downs was obscured by low cloud. In the immediate foreground, though, a large black saloon was winding its way up the long drive from the lodge. 'Here's Cardinal O'Keane's man. I wonder why Montefalco isn't coming.'

'He's probably on his way back from India. And

that's another thing. Frankly, we're bloody lucky nothing happened over there. I think it was a hell of a risk to make the assumptions you did.'

'Well, I was right, and besides, if there had been a plan to make the hit there, our chances of getting on to it were so slim as to be negligible. I was going to send Gallagher and Kelly; I'm rather glad they didn't want to go, because even though the trail's gone tepid for the moment here, we've made a lot of progress.'

'But your man in the AT Squad isn't going to give you any more, is he, and what else have we got to go on?'

'The Manchester connection looks promising, though I think we might be dealing with another branch of the organization. The only common link we've established is the Imam Hafiz Jadid, the religious leader who was staying in Queen's Gate. Unfortunately, I know very little about him or where he's coming from. MI5 have him logged as an ex-member of Islamic Jihad, but that's all.'

The official car from the Papal nunciate had disappeared from view round the side of the house and a few moments later, Bowring and Dowson were interrupted by a knock on the door, followed by Miss MacFarlane announcing, 'Father Sullivan,' and showing in a short man wearing a dog-collar and a well-cut black suit.

Father Sullivan was in his forties, sharp-eyed and with a pugnacity discernible in his manner and his handshake.

When the three men had introduced themselves, Bowring offered drinks.

'Bourbon,' the priest specified in a strong Midwest accent and a way that suggested that, though he might be a man of the cloth, he was also a man of the world.

Bowring waved the American into one of the leather Empire chairs, while he and Dowson sat at each end of the writing-table.

James brought the drinks and poured them. When he'd left, Father Sullivan came straight to the point.

'Look,' he said in a voice that was surprisingly gravelly for his small frame. 'The cardinal wants you guys to pull out of this deal.'

Bowring let neither his surprise nor his exasperation show. 'Pull out? But Father Sullivan, we have established that there are a number of people already in the country almost certainly planning to kill the leader of your church. Surely you can't ignore the seriousness of that threat?'

'We don't think there is a threat any more. We've had information that the plans for the assassination have fallen apart.'

'Where did you get this information?'

'I can't tell you that,' the priest said curtly. 'You know damn well we receive a lot of intelligence through our Middle Eastern legations. For God's sake, it was us who picked up on Sufuf Allah's plan in the first place.'

Dowson leant forward in his chair. 'But Father Sullivan, we have a contract with your government. Unlike the Catholic Church, we are not a charity, and we entered into the contract on the basis that we stood a good chance of earning our performance bonus.'

'Don't worry about that. If His Holiness doesn't get shot, you get your bonus, and all your expenses to date.'

Bowring took a deep breath and leaned back in his

chair. 'You're the client. It's up to you. But I'll want this alteration to your terms in writing.'

Dowson looked at his principal, who deflected him with a glance and went on: 'But until I'm able to assess the quality of your intelligence, I think you'd be very unwise to dispense with our services.'

'Cardinal O'Keane is adamant. He feels we could do ourselves a lot of damage by being involved in this unofficial killing that's been going on.'

'Why? There's absolutely nothing to connect you to it.'

'Except you, Bowring.'

'I'm hardly likely to offer that information to our authorities, or the French.'

'You may not have the choice.'

'Believe me, Father Sullivan,' Bowring said coldly, 'you can have absolutely no doubt that the choice will always be mine. But before I accept your alteration to our agreement, I should like it confirmed directly to me or my representative by your superior.'

'You don't think the cardinal has time to come round to clandestine meetings with mercenaries, do you?'

'Possibly not, but our agent, Mr Dowson here, is quite ready to leave for Rome immediately. So, you arrange it. Then, of course, we'll cease all active involvement at once.'

The priest took a moody swig of his whisky. 'OK,' he said decisively. 'I'll fix it. Just one thing, though. Cardinal O'Keane hasn't had a chance yet to talk about this to Monsignor di Montefalco, who's not back from India yet. If Montefalco gets in touch, just stall him, OK?'

Bowring nodded. 'No problem. But in the meantime, I think you should consider what you're saying. Although the Diplomatic Protection Squad will be in operation as a matter of course, they are not aware as we are of Sufuf Allah's original intentions. Are you going to tell them about this?'

'No point. Like I say, we consider, from the intelligence we have received, that there isn't a risk any more. And we don't want to put any kind of diplomatic strain on His Holiness's visit here.'

Bowring turned to Dowson. 'You'd better get off to Rome then, Michael.'

11

The same dense blanket of cloud which had hidden the South Downs from Bowring's view extended across the rest of England, swallowing up the treeless ridges of Howden Moor.

Kelly peered through his Zeiss 10×50s down into the valley where the brook that was the young River Derwent flowed off the north-eastern flanks of Bleaklow Hill in the High Peak between Sheffield and Manchester.

'Bloody hell,' he said in a husky undertone. 'He'll have to do better than that if he thinks he's going to have a fair crack at the job.'

Michelle was beside him, likewise prostrate in a shallow hide of heather and bracken. They had walked three miles up to the ridge from the next valley. Once they had hit the skyline, Kelly had insisted that they crawl. In a battered bergen, one which he had bought on his trip to Hereford, he had carried a rudimentary camouflage kit.

'You could do better then that,' Kelly added with a laugh.

'I suppose all soldiers are chauvinists by definition,' Michelle observed lightly. 'Even when you know I could probably do better than you.' She also had her glasses trained on the two men who stood amid waist-high bracken, two hundred and fifty yards below them.

One was a dark-skinned Palestinian who'd spent the previous five years being educated at the University in Amman, and in the Bekhar valley. He had learnt to parse an English sentence and strip down an AK47 with equal facility. Now he was teaching, not English, but the handling of small arms to his English pupil.

Kelly and Michelle had heard enough about this Englishman to feel they were beginning to know him.

Michael Duckett, born and brought up in Wandsworth, South London, abandoned at the age of six and taken in by Barnardos, had eventually won a place at Westminster Polytechnic to read Economics and History. But he had never reconciled himself to his early abandonment. His burning resentment had deflected the few people who had ever made any attempt to like this unlikeable boy. When it had been expounded to him by an Islamic fundamentalist group in the Poly, he had hungrily grasped to his bosom the notion of universal Muslim brotherhood. He was deeply grateful to belong, grateful to the point of being ready to risk his life to demonstrate his commitment.

But even if he was prepared to die hitting out at the world's most prominent Infidel, he must do it effectively. He must learn how to place the shots, in quick succession from a distance that was likely to be the closest he would come to his target. And, as his Arab brothers had told him, because he was white he would be able to get much closer than they would.

Duckett felt honoured, and at the same time anxious not to let down his Muslim mentors. He gritted his teeth and clutched the wooden butt of the .375 Colt he had acquired two days before in a tacky bar in Moss Side. Ahmed Qureshi had been there in the bar to watch the negotiations.

Qureshi had not seen the gun, or the money, but he knew Duckett was there to do a deal, and that he wasn't buying crack.

Kelly and Michelle, outside the bar, had watched him walk back to his digs up the Oxford Road. After that, one of the three of them had stayed near him for the next forty-eight hours, until, that morning, he'd been picked up by a young Arab in a new BMW and driven out of Manchester on the M67, through Glossop and up into the High Peak by the Snake Pass.

Qureshi had followed and reported back when the BMW had turned up the small road to the Howden Reservoir, deep in the upper Derwent valley.

They had tried to guess the purpose of Duckett's journey there. And Kelly had worked out from the map where the two men might have gone.

Duckett and his trainer had chosen as isolated a spot as they could have found on a grey Tuesday morning. They had brought with them a bagful of empty Coca-Cola cans, now lined up on a rock ledge twenty yards from where they stood in the bracken.

The pistol was silenced, though Kelly could make out another weapon in the Palestinian's hand – an airgun, probably, to explain their activity to any possible, though unlikely, passer-by.

Duckett reloaded and fired another six rounds in quick succession. This time he hit two of the cans, an improvement on his previous best score of one.

'He's very nervous,' Kelly whispered.

'How can you tell?'

'From the way he's standing; he's much too uptight.'

They watched him load and empty the six chambers a dozen more times. He was beginning to show more consistency.

'If he gets near enough, and he's not too worried about getting caught, he could do damage,' Kelly pointed out.

'Then we should get rid of him now, surely,' Michelle whispered back.

'No. They'll have a back-up. The only way to be sure they fail is to be there when he's about to make the hit. They'll have no time to replace him then. Right, we've seen enough of this. We'll try and get back to the car before they leave.'

Kelly led the way, flat on his belly up to the ridge, staying in the bracken so that the hump of his bergen wouldn't show.

On the other side, they stopped a moment for Kelly to raise Qureshi on the walkie-talkie.

'We're coming back down to our car now. We may get there before them, in which case we'll wait. But you stay in yours on the main road. They'll probably head back to Manchester. Stick with them until you know we're on to them, then we'll have to leap-frog. And get Bowring on the phone and tell him we need at least three more men up here.'

Kelly had parked the Astra twenty feet into the woods off a hairpin in the road and thrown a camouflage net over it.

The two men in the BMW following the lane down the side of the reservoir to the main road wouldn't have seen it, even if they'd been looking. Michelle and Kelly watched them go past.

'We'll leave Qureshi to pick them up first,' said Kelly. He squelched his radio to raise the journalist and told him to be ready for them. Qureshi was waiting a hundred and fifty yards east of the junction with the road that snaked across the bare hills from Sheffield.

'Men, I asked for,' Kelly said to Haynes. 'And he sends his old nanny.'

Haynes laughed. 'You don't want to worry about her. She knows what she's doing; he's trained her himself. And no one ever susses they're being watched by an old lady like that.'

Michelle, Kelly and Haynes were in Kelly's bedroom in the Piccadilly Hotel. Miss MacFarlane and Gallagher were taking a four-hour watch outside the large, gloomy house where Duckett had taken digs.

'I hope you're bloody right. The Pope arrives tomorrow, goes to Buck House; next day, Westminster Cathedral; Saturday, private audiences; Sunday, mass in Cardiff; Tuesday, Aintree.'

'Where do you think our man will try his hit?' Haynes asked.

'Could be any of them, though as he's up here, and his back-up, I'd say Aintree was favourite.'

'Yeah, that's what the boss thought, too,' Gallagher said, nodding. 'Especially as you didn't find any real heavy Muslim militant groups in Cardiff. Buck House trip's no good; he goes by too fast and disappears into the palace. And matey wouldn't risk trying to go into the Cathedral with a weapon, would he?'

'No. His best chance is definitely one of the open-air gigs – Liverpool or Hyde Park. But it makes no odds.

Provided we don't lose him, we'll know where he's going for it.'

Bowring met his London agent in Dowson's house in Lord North Street, near the Houses of Parliament.

'Well?'

'O'Keane's adamant there's no threat – at least, not enough to justify the risk of us getting tangled up with our own security services. I think he's having a dose of cold feet about employing us in the first place.'

'Why should he get cold feet now, for God's sake?'

'I don't know; he didn't tell me and I'm not a mind-reader. I suspect his diplomatic colleagues got wind of it and are kicking up a fuss.'

'What's he like, then?'

'Big, tough bastard; more like a fight promoter than a cardinal, though I gather he's on the liberal wing of the Catholic Church.'

'He's wrong about the absence of a threat. Kelly and this chap Qureshi are on to an Englishman, a crank called Michael Duckett who's become a fanatical Muslim. He's already got a record for ABH at an anti-Salman Rushdie rally. He was in contact with Jadid before he disappeared, and he's been buying weapons and taking shooting lessons from an ex-PLO soldier.'

'Where is he now?'

'Manchester.'

'Aintree, do you think?'

'No guarantee. I've got five watchers on him at the moment, plus Qureshi, who's pretty useful. They'll know soon enough when Duckett makes his move.'

'Aren't you going to call them off, now I've got

confirmation of the revised terms from the cardinal?'

Bowring shook his head. 'No, I'm not. It's possible that Duckett and whoever's put him up to it aren't part of Sufuf Allah, but I think it very likely there's at least a connection through the Imam Jadid. Besides, I'm not sure about O'Keane's motives, and I want to be sure we get our performance bonus.'

'What are you implying about O'Keane, exactly?'

'I'm not sure. But apart from any financial considerations, as you well know, once I've taken on a job. I'm very disinclined to drop it; it's not good for our reputation.'

'You won't get any more exes paid from now on,' said Dowson, whose fees in part depended on the profitability of a job.

'But if His Holiness goes home walking in his own white leather slippers, we get a million dollars; seems worth a small investment to make certain of it.'

'As a matter of curiosity, Piers, do you have any personal feelings about saving the Pope's life?'

Bowring lifted his shoulders. 'He seems a perfectly nice chap, with sound views on homosexuals, but I'm C of E myself.'

Dowson burst out laughing. 'Who are you kidding? You're not C of anything.'

His Holiness John Paul II was greeted with rapturous cheers by a seething crowd outside Buckingham Palace. Interspersed among the crowd were several hundred alert, hard-faced men, too busy to cheer. Special Branch and the Diplomatic Protection Squad had been deployed in strength.

Certain people in M15 and the Anti-Terrorist

Squad had deduced, without firm intelligence, that a new militant fundamentalist Muslim faction was planning an introductory propaganda coup.

The problem was that every known activist of that persuasion who had recently entered the country had ducked clean out of sight. Mick Jones reckoned he was owed a quid pro quo by his old boss; Bowring was stonewalling, claiming he'd lost them too. But Mick knew they had to be still here; no one had seen them leave.

In the isolation of his quite separate department, Harry Cotterell felt cheated by his old friend, but he had nothing to bargain with. He didn't want to fall out with Bowring – God knew, he could have had Piers's hide if he'd wanted – but he was damned if Bowring's gang of hirelings were going to upstage his own department.

In Manchester, Kelly and his team had scattered themselves around several small hotels, and restricted their meetings to cells of two. They only had one tail to watch, and if they lost that, they had no other tracks to follow. Even though they hadn't been sussed, they couldn't afford the smallest risk to their cover.

Miss MacFarlane in her silver Metro proved invaluable, while Michelle's striking looks had to be disguised with spectacles, straggly hair and the dowdiest clothes she could find in the local Oxfam shop.

'Christ, you look terrible,' Kelly said when he saw her.

'Maybe that'll stop you thinking you want to get me into bed all the time.'

'What the hell are you talking about? I've never even suggested it.'

Michelle laughed in a way that instantly neutralized Kelly's annoyance at his own transparency.

'Oh well, if it isn't true, then of course, I apologize.'

'Well,' Kelly said. 'I don't now.'

'I won't look like this for ever, you know.'

Over the next four days neither Duckett nor any of his half-dozen Arab colleagues behaved as if they thought they were being watched. They appeared supremely confident of their cover, all attached as they were in one way or another to the University. Kelly guessed that if they were connected with the heavyweights of Sufuf Allah, the link was fairly remote; certainly none of the 'Joshua Reynolds' appeared in Manchester. Not, that is, until the day before the Pope was due to say Mass at a rally of two hundred thousand Liverpudlian Catholics in the middle of the world's most famous racecourse.

It was Michelle who made the connection, almost by chance as she was just finishing a surveillance stint outside the hall of residence where Duckett and his Muslim brothers most often gathered. Kelly had agreed with Bowring that, through lack of manpower, they wouldn't be able to watch any of Duckett's collaborators, but Michelle, in a newly hired Ford Fiesta, had spotted the Arab whom she and Kelly had watched coaching Duckett out on the moors.

The man got into his BMW and drove, with Michelle close but discreetly behind, a few miles south to Stockport. In the old centre of the town, he parked in a dingy side street and walked into a scruffy restaurant called the Scheherazade Lebanese Kebab House.

Michelle drove on past, parked the car in the next street and, pulling up the collar of her well-worn, ankle-length man's raincoat, sauntered dreamily down the far side of the street. She lost the rhythm of her walk for only a fraction of a second when she saw the Palestinian come out again, look up and down the street, paying her no attention and speaking to someone over his shoulder. A second later Abdul abu Said appeared behind him, and they walked together to the BMW and got in.

Michelle didn't dare turn at once, let alone run back to her car. She could only look in frustration as the car screeched off and turned out of sight. As soon as they were gone, she tried to raise Kelly on her walkie-talkie. But she was out of range; there was no response.

Incensed at her bad luck in getting caught out, she turned back. She forced herself to stay at the same dozy pace, in case anyone was watching from the restaurant, ambled back to the corner, then ran to her car.

There was just a chance she might catch up with them if they were heading back into Manchester.

But she didn't.

Fifteen minutes later, she burst into Kelly's room in a small hotel in Lever Street.

'What the hell are you doing here?' he asked.

'I've just seen Abdul abu Said, with one of Duckett's friends.'

Kelly jumped to his feet.

'Shit! Where?'

'I followed the PLO man, the one who was training Duckett, down to a kebab place in Stockport. I left my car, and saw him come back out with this other guy

– definitely Abdul abu Said, I'm sure of it. But they drove off fast and I couldn't catch them.'

'Bloody hell, I wish we had more men! They must be going for the hit at Aintree tomorrow and this guy's come up to take charge.'

'I think so.'

'Right! We can't let Duckett out of our sight. The five of us, and Qureshi, we'll have to put a six-man watch on him, to cover the back entrance of anywhere he goes. He's going to be a lot more nervous and careful now it's so close. Especially if abu Said's here now; he's not going to take any chances, and he knows how to keep out of sight. You get on to Miss MacFarlane and Terry and tell them what's going on. They're to join up with Andy and Qureshi. I'll talk to the boss and catch up with you. Make sure Andy and Terry have a few spare magazines, too.'

'And me,' Michelle said coolly.

'Yeah, sure, you too.'

Bowring put the phone down, pleased with himself. He'd got his men in the right place at the right time – a fundamental prerequisite for success in battle. They knew what to do at Aintree, and how to do it.

However, he hadn't expected any known representatives of Sufuf Allah to turn up there. But if they were involved, they were unlikely to be deterred by one failure and the loss of one English Muslim. Quite probably, they were prepared to treat the thing as a dummy run if it didn't come off.

He looked out of his library window for a few moments at the beeches in his woods, turned to gold now by the sinking sun. He reached forward and picked up the phone again. He dialled a number and listened thoughtfully to its ringing. When it was answered, he spoke quietly.

'We start watching tomorrow. Confirm the rooms and have everyone in place by midday.'

'OK, sir.'

'I'll let you know how to contact me in the morning. Be available to take my call at eight-thirty.'

'Understood, sir.'

Kelly was right. Having been a basic, simple task, the surveillance had now become more complicated. Suddenly Duckett and his supporters seemed to have been made aware of the possibility that they were being watched, for they had taken to moving around separately and using alternative exits to the buildings they entered. Kelly, in no doubt now that Duckett was to be the hit man despite his inexperience, concentrated his restricted manpower on the Englishman.

The next morning Gallagher watched Duckett walk a short way down the Oxford Road, turn off, and get into a small Ford van which he hadn't used before. As Kelly and his team had expected, the van headed west out of Manchester on the M62. Between them, the SOS task force had five inconspicuous vehicles: two driven by single women and one by a scruffily dressed Asian. Haynes went with Kelly to co-ordinate communications.

Duckett surprised them by not turning north on to the M57, but then he'd almost certainly been told to be careful.

Kelly got on the radio. 'Brenda and Qureshi, stay with him. We'll get on up and wait on the A59 on the way out. Give me any significant direction changes.'

From the bulletins issued every so often by Miss

MacFarlane and Qureshi, Duckett drove on into central Liverpool to make a few inept attempts to shake any tail before he inevitably headed north for Aintree.

More significant was Miss MacFarlane's next report. 'He's picked up some support.'

'Switch channels to specify,' Kelly snapped.

She came back on a new wavelength. 'I've seen two. A blind mouse and got no knickers.'

'Thanks, Brenda,' he laughed.

He cut off and turned to Haynes in the driver's seat. 'Did you get that? Registration letters ABM and GNK. Neither of those is local, so with luck we won't get on to a red herring. Anyway, I should get the numbers from her later.'

Kelly wasn't surprised that Duckett had back-up, but he doubted that they would keep too close to him when they reached the racecourse, if they went in at all. At least SOS would be ready for them.

There was a steady stream of traffic with them on the motorway now, a lot of it, Kelly guessed, heading for the Papal rally. Once they had turned off to follow the signs to Aintree, cars and coaches were converging from every direction, eventually bottle-necking in the approaches to the car parks.

Kelly called Gallagher on the radio.

'Carry on and pick them up on their way up the A59. Keep in vision, then take close order. Report your position before you leave your car.'

'Roger.'

'You too, *chérie*.'

Kelly watched Gallagher and Michelle overtake them and carry on past the entrance to the racecourse. Despite the density of the traffic, he didn't think they would have too much trouble picking out the white van and Qureshi and Miss MacFarlane's cars. With luck they would also identify Duckett's back-up from the registrations.

Haynes drove the Astra where they were directed into the main car park, to the west of the stands. He parked, and stayed in the car. Kelly got out, wearing his headset, as if he were listening to the live radio commentary of the event, and a hidden throat mike. Round his neck, like many another experienced rally-goer, hung a pair of binoculars. He wandered back towards the entrance and leant against a fence post to watch the crowds flock in to pay their respects to the leader of the world's most numerous religion.

Haynes's voice fizzed in his headphones. 'Brenda's given me the numbers, I've relayed them to Andy.'

Five minutes later he came on again more urgently. 'Andy's followed matey round to the car park on the other side, by the Canal Turn. So did his back-up.'

Kelly pushed himself off his fence post and started to walk with the rest of the crowd through the main gates behind the old grandstand.

Out in the centre of the course, a vast platform had been erected, facing the stands. It was eight feet high, some sixty feet long and thirty deep, to accommodate the Pope, his entourage and Britain's leading Catholics. At the back of the platform, on its own dais, was set a large, neo-gothic throne beside an altar with all the paraphernalia of crucifixes, lecterns, candles, thuribles, and bells, as well as microphones to relay the words of the Mass through banks of loudspeakers dotted among the already vast crowd.

Kelly climbed a short way, as far as he could, up the steps of the stands, which were jammed full by then. He gazed with frustration across a sea of heads to a point on the far side of the course where thousands more were pouring into the area ringed by the racetrack.

The excited murmur of the crowd was joined by the music of a brass band accompanying the opening hymns. Kelly came back down from the stand, muttering as he went, 'Terry, I'm going to try and make it across, but tell Andy he's on his own.'

Gallagher parked his car twenty feet from Duckett's van. He put on his Walkman headphones and turned up his collar. To comply with Bowring's explicit orders, he wasn't carrying his Browning, but tucked inside his denim jacket in a tough, slim leather sheath was a freshly honed, nine-inch stiletto of dark steel.

He got out of the car, and his flesh tingled at the sight of his target within easy calling distance. He looked around, smiling affably at anyone and everyone, to show that he was sharing in the excitement and goodwill of the occasion.

Duckett's bony features were pale, framed by his lank brown hair. Gallagher could almost feel the tension in him now his Muslim brothers had left him on his own to make his grand gesture for Islam. Certainly there were no Middle Eastern faces in the crowd immediately around him.

Duckett carefully locked his van and began to walk stiffly with everyone else in the direction of the huge platform, four hundred yards away.

Gallagher slipped in behind him, never more than twenty feet away, but always with at least half a dozen people between them.

Duckett did glance back now and then, nervously

and not expecting to see any face he recognized, not really seeing at all. Gallagher carefully avoided his eyes, mingling with the people closest to him, exchanging pleasantries with them.

As they got closer to the platform where Catholic dignitaries in white vestments were beginning to gather, the crowd became denser, but not impassable, as people had seated themselves on the ground on rugs or on small collapsible chairs, unscrewing vacuum flasks of tea and waving banners of welcome for the Pope.

Duckett wormed his way deeper into the throng, drawing closer to the platform where shortly His Holiness Pope John Paul II would arrive to give his first blessing to the great gathering. He stopped beneath a cluster of loudspeakers, and leant against the scaffold tower that held them.

Gallagher hung back for a moment before taking a wide arc to approach the tower a little in front of Duckett, but keeping out of his direct line of sight.

The people were all singing now, in the ragged disharmony of an outdoor congregation. Gallagher mimed along to it as he slowly worked his way to the scaffold tower, until he was on the other side of it to Duckett, with barely eight feet separating them.

They were fifty feet from the platform, well within the range of Duckett's competence with a gun. This was undoubtedly going to be his point of fire. What the Scot had to judge was how soon after the Pope's appearance, Duckett would take his shot.

His Holiness had been driven through a well-stewarded gap to the back of the dais. As he appeared, with the sun gleaming off his white garments and skullcap, the crowd gave a thunderous cheer and surged forward a few feet, Duckett with them.

Gallagher took his chance and slipped round the scaffold poles until he was two feet from the hit man, jostling shoulders on either side. All eyes except his were fixed on the shining figure of the frail septuagenarian on the platform above them.

Duckett stood stock-still, transfixed, it seemed, by this first sight of his target, unconscious of the people closely packed around him. Gallagher's eyes didn't leave him for a second as he watched for a movement. Surreptitiously he slipped on a pair of gloves and felt inside his jacket for the narrow hilt of his weapon. He drew it slowly from its sheath.

As soon as Duckett's right shoulder moved, as his hand went to grasp the gun in his pocket, Gallagher closed the gap between them to a few inches, but still not touching Duckett or doing anything that might alert him or disturb his concentration. He undid the three copper buttons of his jacket and waited until the gun was about to be pulled into view.

As soon as Duckett's hand had emerged from his pocket, Gallagher leant back slightly. In a single, continuous movement, he pulled out the thin blade, held it parallel to the ground at chest height and pushed himself forward.

He felt the man tremble and gasp, though any sounds he made were drowned by the roar of welcoming cheers all round. No one except Gallagher saw the gun fall from the white, bony fingers. He bent down and quickly stuffed it in his pocket.

As the man crumpled, Gallagher, leaving the handle of the stiletto protruding from his back, took hold of

him beneath his shoulders and lowered him solicitously to the ground, where he propped him against
the scaffold tower.

A few people on either side glanced down with
fleeting concern at a man who had obviously found
the excitement of the event too much. Gallagher
didn't look up; he crouched in front of the stricken
man and talked to him. 'Wait here, Jimmy. I'll go and
find a doctor.'

The sound of the Pope's characteristically accented
English boomed from the loudspeakers above, while
everyone hung on to each word of his greeting.

Gallagher stood up. 'I'll be right back,' he said to
the corpse in front of him.

He squeezed his way through the crowd, who were
now intently muttering the Lord's Prayer. 'Forgive us
our trespasses . . .'

As Gallagher smiled apologetically and shoved his
way towards the car park, he wondered if he would be
forgiven this trespass. Or could it be deemed a trespass
at all to have killed a man about to kill the Pope.

Kelly stood at the back of the gathering on some
railings, muttering the prayers of his childhood out
of ineradicable habit, angrily scrutinizing the sea of
heads through his binoculars for any sign of Duckett,
Gallagher or anyone else involved in his operation.

The Pope had been visible for fifteen minutes
now and Mass was about to begin, when he would
move from the front of the dais, further back to
the altar.

Presumably Duckett knew this. He must have
watched what happened at the other open-air events.
Maybe he had chickened out at the last minute – it

often happened with amateurs. Or maybe he hadn't been able to get within range.

A short burst on a St John's Ambulance siren made itself heard above the sound of hymn-singing and the brass band. Kelly turned sharply to watch the ambulance head into a mass of slowly moving people to his right. He held his breath. Maybe, he thought fervently, Gallagher had got there and Duckett was already dead. He swung his binoculars to the left, towards the Canal Turn, where the two of them had parked. But it was useless; he couldn't pick out any individual at that distance.

Haynes's voice in his earphones took him by surprise.

'Andy's leaving.'

'Has he done the repair job he was supposed to?'

'Yeah, no more trouble there.'

'Good. Tell everyone to go south. I'll see you in a few minutes.'

Kelly picked up Haynes's copy of the *Sun* from the passenger seat and chucked it in the back. He got in, closed the door and gave his signaller a big grin.

'We cracked it, then.'

'Andy was bloody sure of it. Sounded very pleased with himself.'

'Where is he now?'

'He'll be on the motorway.'

'What about the others?'

'Michelle and Brenda were watching his back-up. They stayed outside, didn't move.'

'Did they recognize any of them?'

'I think so, but we were being careful, of course.

I think Michelle was trying to say it was the geezer who took matey out for his target practice.'

'What about Abdul abu Said?'

'Nah. They didn't say so, anyway.'

'I wonder where the hell he was, then.'

'Well, wherever he was, he didn't get in Andy's way. Are you going to tell the boss?'

'Not over the mobile, not here. Too risky. I'll do it from a call-box later. Now, let's try and catch the others up. We'll have to think of somewhere for a pull-in.'

The SOS team, minus the temporarily seconded Qureshi, met up in a large, noisy pub on the outskirts of Oxford. Kelly felt safer south of Birmingham. He bought the drinks, then went to phone Bowring.

He came back from delivering the good news looking subdued. 'Sorry, we've got to move. The boss wants a briefing in two hours at HQ.'

12

'For some reason, somebody's decided to sit on it,' Bowring said. 'There's been nothing on the news or Ceefax about a fatality at Aintree, though they must have had him in hospital nearly four hours ago.' He turned to Gallagher. 'You're absolutely certain you neutralized him?'

'Aye, course I am. No question about it. I put the blade straight through his heart. He'd stopped breathing by the time I left him.'

'Hmm. Even if his back-up don't know he's dead yet, they certainly know he didn't shoot the Pope.'

Bowring was sitting on the writing-table in his library at Summerfold House. His eclectic band of mercenaries sat scattered around the room in a state of exhaustion. None of them had slept for thirty-six hours. He had congratulated them handsomely enough on their success, but made it clear that they had won only half the battle.

'With Abdul abu Said involved and over here, it's unlikely that he'll leave without trying another hit, and he's still got a prime opportunity the day after tomorrow in London. I've already put a very expensive surveillance exercise into operation along the vulnerable parts of the Pope's route, so all of you are going back to London tonight, except Miss MacFarlane, who's had enough excitement for one day. You're all booked into Londonderry House; it's the closest we could get.'

'But boss, you don't think they'll try another hit from the crowd, do you?'

'No, I didn't before, and I certainly don't now – not after they failed at Aintree. Frankly, if I'd been them, I'd have gone along with the Duckett plan, hoping but not really expecting it to work. I'd certainly have had a more substantial scheme worked out as a fall-back. So, we know they're here, and we know they mean business.'

Bowring looked at each of his employees, assessing their state of mind and fitness. Apparently satisfied, he said: 'Now, there's some food being prepared for you before you leave. I'll continue the briefing over dinner. I think in the meantime, you might be permitted a bath – in Michelle's case, that's an order; pity we haven't got a decent wig for you – and a glass or two of champagne.' He picked up his phone, pressed a button and said: 'James, a few bottles of Cristal, please.'

When James appeared, sooner than expected, he wasn't carrying champagne. There was a look of consternation on his stony face.

'Excuse me, sir. There's been a break in the perimeter circuit.'

Bowring glanced at him sharply. 'Where?'

'Somewhere up by the top of the hill behind the house.'

'Terry, get up to the monitors at once and check all the systems.'

Haynes was already on his feet, his fatigue overcome by the adrenalin rush as he left the room at a run.

Bowring then turned to Kelly. 'Is there any chance there was a tail on you back here?'

'No way. We left Duckett's back-up facing the wrong way and looking in the wrong direction.' He looked at Michelle. 'Isn't that right?'

'Sure, if those two cars were his only back-up.'

'But,' said Miss MacFarlane, speaking for the first time since coming into the house, 'we didn't see abu Said there, and I feel sure he must have been in the vicinity.'

'Yes,' Bowring nodded. 'That's right. Michelle, you saw him only once, leaving the restaurant in Stockport?'

She nodded her greasy, spiky head. 'Then I'm afraid I lost him. I never saw where the Palestinian took him.'

The telephone on Bowring's table trilled. It was Haynes in the communications room. 'Boss, we're picking up human movement from two of the MAGIDs.' That meant armed humans.

Bowring banged the phone down and jumped to his feet. 'We've got visitors. You must have been watched coming back from Liverpool; that means they know about The Hollies. All of you come up to the signals room; I'll brief you there.'

Up in the attic, surrounded by the radios, receivers, and CCTV monitors, Bowring checked the position. Haynes, with headphones on, was picking up something on the acoustic buoys hanging in the trees. 'I just got a whisper, couldn't understand it, sounded like Arabic.'

'There's two moving up on The Hollies, boss,' Kelly said, staring at the monitor from the television camera mounted on the villa's roof.'

'There are at least six more in the woods,' Haynes added urgently.

'Right,' Bowring said calmly. 'We're definitely about to come under attack. Kelly, Andy, Michelle and Terry, arm up lightly, use your headsets. Miss MacFarlane, take over the radio. James, get on the roof with an L96 with a night-scope. They won't come on until the light's completely gone. That gives us half an hour for you four to get down to the ice house and deploy in two groups up around the inside of the fence. Jack, you and Michelle take the western perimeter; Andy and Terry, come up the east side of the house to the top of the hill and circle back down towards it. Move in and neutralize any enemy as you find them. And be quiet about it. I don't want the locals calling the police. You'll have the advantage, since Brenda can give you their positions and they won't be expecting you from behind. Now, go.'

Haynes had already relinquished his place to Miss MacFarlane. Kelly led him, Gallagher and Michelle down the stairs to the armoury. They blacked up and slipped on battle smocks and belts. They each took a Browning and fitted a silencer; Kelly and Gallagher also took Colt Commandos, as weapons of last resort, with braces of magazines taped end to end. When they had pulled on their headsets they ran through the cellars and the brick door, down to the well room.

Kelly flashed his torch down the well and swung himself over the side to grab the iron rungs. The others followed and they swarmed down the shaft until the opening into a horizontal tunnel showed up in Kelly's torch beam.

It was similar in size and construction to the one

from The Hollies and they barely had to crouch to run its three-hundred-yard length. At the far end, Michelle knew the mechanism for getting through into the ice house. Before they stepped through the door, Kelly reiterated Bowring's orders. He and Michelle would take the west flank of the woods. The other two would take the east, which was the quickest way up the hill, to come back down towards the rear of the house.

In the signals room, Bowring stood behind Miss MacFarlane. On the VDU in front of her was a map of the grounds, showing the position of each surveillance device that had been triggered.

Only one breach in the perimeter wire was showing, but the pattern of disturbances from the seismic and acoustic monitors showed that the intruders had split into three or possibly four groups.

Bowring was staring now at the CCTV monitors banked above the VDU. The cameras were fitted with light-intensifying lenses which amplified whatever ambient light remained in the woodland dusk. One of them had picked up two shadowy figures who had stopped within its field of vision.

They appeared to have settled down to wait, confirming Bowring's view that the attack would not start for a while yet. But every few seconds his eyes flashed back to the monitor from the camera covering The Hollies' entrance to the tunnel. He hoped the two men who had come into the house would search it thoroughly enough to find the tunnel.

Excluding these two men, he assessed that his four soldiers out in the grounds were outnumbered two to one. With the element of surprise and regular position information from Miss MacFarlane, he could live with those odds. In addition, he and James were in a position to pick off any who came within sight of the house.

'OK, Nanny, I'm going next door to the window overlooking the stable block.' He picked up a walkie-talkie and an L96 which James had brought up for him. He checked the magazine, nodded at Miss MacFarlane and walked through the attic to the back of the house, where a small mansard window in what was once a maid's room gave him a view of the wooded hill behind and the cluster of outbuildings that had housed his ancestor's horses and carriage.

Kelly and Michelle worked their way through the gathering gloom of night, through the patchy woodland at the edge of Summerfold House's boundary. Kelly was glad now of the day he had spent in these woods checking and installing systems, although, at the time, it had seemed a very remote possibility that he would have to fight in them.

Miss MacFarlane quietly relayed over his headphones each new piece of intelligence provided by the network of surveillance devices and the TV cameras.

Kelly had a clear picture of the map of the grounds in his head and even in the darkening conditions was fairly sure of their own position.

'There are two men in vision, five yards west of camera two,' Miss MacFarlane's soft Scottish voice came through his headphones. 'There are two or three more twenty yards due south of them, currently static.'

Kelly knew where he was in relation to camera two. They were well placed to hit the other group of three. He signalled Michelle to stop behind him and indicated that they were going to take a right angle eastwards into the woods. He spaced them fifteen feet apart and started forward. At first the ground cover was sparse. They flitted from tree to tree to cover thirty yards before they came up against a mountainous bank of rhododendrons. When they stopped and slipped their headphones off to listen, they caught a few faint sounds of movement, the crunch of a human foot on woodland detritus that no native animal could have made. They were no more than twenty feet away, on the far side of the gigantic shrub.

Kelly replaced his headphones, to hear the message: 'The two men by camera two have moved off towards the east . . . They're now giving readings north-east on seismic seven.'

Kelly racked his brains for the location of seismic seven. He calculated from the sequence of numbers that it was about three hundred yards from his present position. That left them a clear field to deal with whoever was in front of them. But he wished he knew how many there were. He slipped his phones off and indicated to Michelle that she should go round the far side of the bush, so they would hit them on two flanks.

Pausing between each step, they slowly arced round until they were on the point of coming into sight of their targets. Inch by inch, Kelly brought his head round until he could make out three dim figures standing in a small clearing with their backs to him, peering intently through the trees towards the open lawn in front of the house. The nearest man to him stood alone, a few yards from his colleagues – like a lamb on the edge of the flock, Kelly thought.

He withdrew and devised an instant plan. Silently,

without even a creak of his bones, he lowered himself to a crouch and picked up a stout, two-foot length of dead beech. He straightened himself and with his left hand pulled his knife from the sheath on his belt. He stretched his other arm behind him, clutching the short branch, and swung it up and over like a cricketer throwing the ball in from the outfield.

He aimed his projectile between the trees in front of him and it flew in a silent parabola beyond the enemy to land with a noisy crash and a thud on the ground thirty feet ahead of them. They started, and one of them muttered something as they tried to see what had caused the disturbance.

Kelly transferred his hunting knife to his right hand and stole across the few feet that separated him from the nearest man, hoping that Michelle would take the cue. Three strides took him to just behind his target. The broad blade of his knife was slicing through the gristle of the man's windpipe before he knew he'd been attacked. As he fell to the ground with a last cough, his comrades swung round, momentarily disorientated, staring sightlessly into the gloom.

Kelly dropped his knife and reached for the Browning at his belt. Before he had drawn it, the next man was swinging an AK47 towards him. The Arab hadn't completed his turn when two muffled coughs of a silenced handgun carried across the clearing and he froze in mid-turn, jerked again and pitched headlong into the undergrowth, crunching his ribs on the butt of his rifle.

As he fell, another double-tap from the bushes to Kelly's right took out the third man while he was still trying to work out what was happening.

Kelly had got his own gun out now. He stepped

across to the fallen men and quickly put two more shots into each of the three bodies. Bowring's orders had been to neutralize the enemy, which meant making sure they wouldn't pick up a weapon again, ever.

Michelle walked into the gloom of the clearing, slipping her Browning back into a webbing pouch on her belt.

Kelly put his headphones on again.

'There is movement by acoustic buoy one, one hundred feet due north of the coach-house,' Miss MacFarlane was intoning. That was Gallagher's territory.

Kelly turned towards Michelle and put his mouth to her ear. 'Thanks, pal,' he breathed and turned to head up towards the two men last monitored at seismic seven.

Bowring had ordered one-way radio traffic to avoid the slightest temptation to any of his men on the ground to give themselves away. But the lack of incoming information was frustrating. He heard Miss MacFarlane give the position of the enemy a hundred feet above the house. One of his patrols ought to have been behind them. Holding his L96 lightly at the ready, he strained his ears and eyes into the last remnants of daylight.

Miss MacFarlane's voice came through the receiver clipped to the lapel of his jacket: 'Tunnel entry camera showing enemy intrusion . . .'

Bowring put down his gun and walked briskly back to the signal room. He arrived there in time to see activity on the last monitor. Two soldiers, clearly lit by the lights in the cellar at The Hollies, were trying to open the door to the tunnel. He couldn't see their faces, but he could see they were well loaded – dressed in DPM combat gear with a belt full of knives, grenades and ammo pouches. He smiled to himself; not unexpectedly, they weren't carrying respirators. He held his breath until they found the switch which unlocked the door and let it swing freely into the tunnel.

They stepped through the doorway and out of sight.

Bowring made himself wait a few more seconds to be sure they were in and going on. When he was satisfied that they were, he leant in front of Miss MacFarlane and pressed three switches in quick succession.

'They're in the trap now,' he said bluntly.

The steel shutters at either end of the tunnel slid into place; and the choke closed on the air-shaft.

Bowring gave Miss MacFarlane a quick glance of justification and flicked a red switch at the side of the console.

They didn't hear the small explosion, deep in the ground beneath them, which transmitted its shock wave down the detonation cord which ran the length of the tunnel. At almost imperceptible intervals, six charges were activated, producing small blasts which impacted through the confined brick tube, releasing clouds of oxygen-devouring red phosphorus.

Gallagher and Haynes had the two intruders behind the house in sight, silhouetted against a solitary light that glowed from the old stable-yard and filtered through the trees. Gallagher guessed that the terrorists were waiting for an order, or a sign, to launch their attack. According to the bulletins from Miss MacFarlane, they were the only enemy on this side of the house. Whatever strategy these Islamic warriors had, it had to be very sketchy, with no maps or plans of the house to go by.

Gallagher nudged his colleague and pulled his Browning from its holster. He had a Colt Commando slung across his chest, but that was only to be used in an extreme emergency. He beckoned Haynes to come with him and started moving soundlessly across a soft floor of pine needles towards their target.

It was a soft thud, deep in the earth beneath them, that distracted Gallagher, momentarily but long enough to let him miss a thick, protruding root of the large ornamental deodar round which he had been creeping. The Arabs heard the explosion too, instantly on their guard, alert to the thump and rattle of the Scot hitting the ground with his weapons. They spun round, both wearing night-vision goggles, AK47s cocked and ready.

Haynes, behind his fallen comrade, had barely acknowledged the crisis before a burst of 5.45mm high-power rounds ripped into him, jerking him like a scarecrow in a gale as he screamed in pain and fear of death.

Before Haynes hit the ground, Gallagher had rolled behind the broad trunk of the deodar, scrambling to his knees as he grabbed up his sub-machine-gun and brought it around the side of the tree. The weapon spat angrily as he emptied half a magazine into the silhouetted figures, saw them shudder and collapse to the ground, one bellowing with the agony of a blasted abdomen.

A flood of light from a row of five-hundred-watt

halogen lamps set beneath the eaves of the house suddenly bathed the whole place in a stark glow.

Gallagher glanced a few yards to the huddled, lifeless khaki lump which had been his friend. He bit his lip and turned his gun again on the whimpering bodies in front of him, pumping the trigger until the metal bit into the flesh of his finger and the magazine was empty.

Kelly and Michelle were keeping ten to fifteen feet apart as they worked their way across two hundred yards of tangled woodland towards the surveillance device designated seismic seven.

There was no new information from Miss MacFarlane through Kelly's headphones as he moved with a stealth which was second nature to him. He stopped and listened every few yards and picked up small sounds of Michelle's progress, sounds which blended convincingly enough with the woodland's natural creaks and rustles. He couldn't condemn her for them; she hadn't spent the months that he had in the jungles of Borneo, or even the tamer forests of Powys and Ulster, where he had learnt his skills; besides, she'd just saved his life.

Another sound, a low, guttural murmur, reached him on the easterly breeze. He prayed that Michelle had heard it too and would have the sense to stay where she was until he'd gone forward. In the few moments he took to plan his next move, the gentle noises of the wood were abruptly shattered by a burst of powerful automatic fire, somewhere behind the house; and a terrible, agonized scream, answered by a short, sharper discharge.

The bushes a few yards in front of him erupted and

two figures broke cover to run across the wide, open space of Summerfold's lawns. Kelly and Michelle emerged together through a border of large azaleas as the floodlights on the house lit up the ground all round it.

One of the soldiers in front of them drew back his right arm and swung it towards the house. A few seconds later, a shattering blast blew a small crater in the border where the grenade had fallen short of the library window.

A sharp crack echoed between the stately Victorian conifers and monkey-puzzle trees standing on the well-mown lawn, then another. The running figures stopped abruptly – reversed as if tugged back by a bungee cord at their collars.

'Get back in!' Kelly yelled at Michelle.

They dived back together through the tall border of shrubs that fronted the woods and crouched side by side. Kelly heard Michelle's breath coming hard, could almost hear her heart beating.

'That must have been James from the roof,' Kelly whispered. 'He wouldn't have identified us from there.'

Michelle nodded. 'Sure. Thanks.'

They waited. Everything was quiet around the floodlit house. The seconds stretched themselves into minutes; still no movement.

Bowring stood behind Miss MacFarlane at the console in the communications room.

'What do you think?' he asked.

'I don't know, not for sure. The pattern of movements through the systems indicated that they split into three separate groups after they breached the fence. One unit went down to the south-west, another up to the north side of the house, and a third in between them.'

'Judging by the gunfire behind the house, that unit's been neutralized. There was only one burst from their weapons, and two from ours. The middle unit would have been the two men that James took out on the lawn,' Bowring concluded.

'But someone moved up towards them. That might have been one of our patrols, or it might have been theirs.'

'Get them to report in. We'll have to risk it.'

Miss MacFarlane flicked her mike switch and said: 'Come in, Coaltit, and report your position.'

They could hear the gloom in Gallagher's voice. 'Fifty feet north of the stable block. Two enemy accounted for; we've taken one fatality.'

Bowring gritted his teeth and winced.

'Get Kelly,' he said tightly.

'Come in, Wagtail, and give your position.'

'South-western corner of the lawn, due west of the two hit from the house.'

'Have you met any other hostile units?'

'Yes; three men, all accounted for.'

Miss MacFarlane looked at Bowring, who said: 'Tell them to come in via the stable block. It looks as though we've neutralized the attack, but James and I will keep them covered, in case there are any more still on the loose. You keep your eyes fixed on those monitors for any signs of extraneous movement.'

'Control to both units. Come in under cover, via the stable block. The door will be released as you reach it,' said Miss MacFarlane into the mike.

Gallagher listened to the order, aware from it that

the attack on their HQ must have been successfully averted, but unable to feel much elation about it. He heaved Haynes's body over his left shoulder, clutching his automatic rifle in the other, and ran the short distance to the stable-yard, which led through to a door into the back of the house. When he reached the door, the lock was released remotely and he pushed through it with the dead weight of his load.

Kelly and Michelle came in a few minutes later.

The whole team, minus their dead colleague, gathered in a small office at the centre of the house on the ground floor which was Bowring's operations room.

'No movements besides yours have registered on the surveillance monitors for over twenty minutes; I'm sure we've dealt with the immediate problem. Unfortunately some public-spirited citizen heard the firing and alerted the police. Fortunately, I'd pre-empted them with my own call of complaint, but the police will be here any time now, so get out and retrieve the bodies; get them to the ice-house tunnel if you can and we'll deal with them later. Andy, take yours down to the well room; and you'd better put Terry there too for the time being. I'll stall a search for as long as I can but I want no bodies, weapons, or soldiers found here; you'll all just have to lie up in the well room until I come and give you the all-clear. You can't go into The Hollies' tunnel; it's full of red phosphorus and two more of our visitors and it'll take the pumps at least two hours to clear.'

The house was in darkness once again. Only a chink of light showed through the library curtains. Kelly was carrying the second body off the lawn when the sound of a siren reached him, winding up the hilly lanes from the A25. He and Michelle had already heaved their first three victims down to the ice house and dumped them inside the tunnel. Once they had got the next two in, they sat on the floor of the tunnel beside them, sweating and panting heavily.

'Christ, I'd forgotten how much a dead man weighs,' Kelly said. 'Still, we've got time for a rest now. The boss isn't going to get rid of the police in a hurry.'

James helped Gallagher to bring in the two men he had riddled after they had shot Haynes. Neither spoke as they wrapped the bodies in tarpaulins to avoid bloodstains and manhandled them through the cellars to the concealed brick doorway into the well room. Then they laid Haynes's ravaged carcass beside the two dead terrorists, and James left Gallagher alone with the corpses.

The local police sergeant, a natural cynic, and the constable with him were at first impressed by the suave ex-Guards officer who greeted them at the front door of Summerfold House. They'd heard of Summerfold, of course, and the rich family which had occupied it for over a century – apart from the short time it had been the home of the drug-abusing rock star, when it had been a regular target of police raids.

About the current incumbent, the sergeant, like most people in the district, knew very little.

'Come in, Sergeant,' said Bowring. 'Sorry to drag you out, possibly quite unnecessarily, but I did hear some odd noises in the woods near the top of the hill. From my rather out-of-date experience of firearms, it sounded like some kind of automatic rifle.'

'How long ago was this, sir?'

'I told the officer at the station maybe half an hour ago.'

'That concurs with another report we had,' said the sergeant. 'Only they said it sounded like some kind of explosion. Has there been any more since?'

'No. Not a sound. I went out and had a walk around. I didn't see or hear anything else. But I really think you ought to put a search party up through the woods. I'd say fifty men could sweep it in a couple of hours.'

'Fifty men, out at this time of night, for an unconfirmed report of something that sounded like gunfire? There's no way anyone here could sanction that.'

'What?' Bowring said with sharp indignation. 'Who's the senior station officer? I'd like to speak to him, right away.'

This was just the kind of high-handed behaviour the sergeant loathed in members of the so-called upper classes, who always treated the police as if they were their own personal servants.

'That won't be necessary, sir,' he said. 'There's no point in searching this place in the dark. I've posted a man down at your front gate. He'll stay for the rest of the night with a back-up squad car, in case there's any further outbreak,' he added with a hint of disbelieving sarcasm, which pleased Bowring. His face no longer expressed the slight awe with which he had entered the house. 'It's possible, sir, isn't it, that it might be someone after the game?'

'Well,' Bowring said as if the idea hadn't occurred to him before, 'we do put down quite a few pheasant and there are a lot of last year's birds still around. And of course, there are the deer up in the top woods.

Good Lord, you might be right.' He became sterner. 'But poaching's still a crime, Sergeant. Putting one officer on the gate isn't going to catch anyone.'

'Yes, sir. Poaching is still a crime, but it wouldn't justify bringing in a search party of fifty men, in the dark, when the poacher's probably been gone half an hour.'

Bowring looked at him, trying, it seemed, to overcome his exasperation. 'Yes, well, I suppose you're right, but I shall institute a search first thing in the morning, and if I find any evidence and report it, I'll expect immediate action.'

'Yes, of course, sir. Now we'll just have a look around outside. We'll let you know if my superiors decide to put fifty men through the woods tomorrow.' His tone made it clear that there wasn't a hope in hell of that.

Bowring stiffly showed him out and watched as he and the constable walked across the lawns with their torches flashing.

'Let's hope they don't find any spent cartridges, sir,' James's voice came from behind him.

'That's a risk I had to take, but frankly I shouldn't think they'll look hard or long. They're only going into the woods to stop me from complaining to the station superintendent. Get out through the stable block now and collect up what you can from where you picked up the two Arabs. Take a radio and a set of headphones. Miss MacFarlane can tell you if the policemen decide to go that way.'

James came back ten minutes later with a bag of fifty spent 7.62mm and 5.54mm cartridges.

'That's all I could find, sir,' he reported to Bowring.

'That looks about right. Now, we'd better find

out who the hell we've neutralized. Get down into the well room with a Polaroid and photograph the bodies. Then we'll have to dispose of them ourselves. There's no point in bringing Harry Cotterell into this yet. I'll break it to him afterwards, and Mick Jones, if the need arises.'

'I could probably deal with them, sir. Hydrochloric acid should do the trick. But Terry Haynes's relatives might like to bury him properly.'

'I'm sorry to say that I can't let that happen. If we manage to get away with this shoot-out tonight, I don't want there to be any more questions asked by Terry's family about it. He'll have to go missing on a job abroad, in a month or so.'

'I understand, sir.'

Gallagher, Michelle and Kelly, who had all three grown to like the little cockney signaller very much, also understood. But any sense of victory they might have felt after their activities that day was nullified by the loss of a member of their small team.

When seven of the dead terrorists were lined up along one wall of the well room, James photographed them. The police had left after a perfunctory search which, as Bowring had gambled, produced nothing to excite their interest, and he decided it was safe to let his soldiers back up into the house. They didn't change out of their military gear and kept their weapons beside them, in the remote event that Sufuf Allah still had a presence in the grounds. They sat around in the library, eating food prepared by the versatile butler.

'Something went seriously wrong today,' Bowring said as they ate. 'I'm very concerned that you were tailed back here, and we may have done irreparable damage to our cover by allowing a shoot-out in the grounds; we won't know for a few days yet whether or not we've got away with it. I'm blaming no one in particular, but we should never have been traced here.'

'Boss, none of us know how the hell we led them here,' Kelly said. 'We all took the usual evasive actions. Only Miss MacFarlane actually drove up to the house, and frankly I checked her for tails two or three times on the way from Liverpool – there was certainly no one on to her. And we all arrived separately at The Hollies.'

'On the positive side,' Bowring went on, 'you eliminated Duckett, and nine members of Sufuf Allah, assuming the two who found their way into the tunnel at The Hollies are dead. I think we've probably accounted for a large proportion of the enemy. Of the original five faces Cotterell gave us, three were killed outside. Maybe the other two are in the tunnel; we'll be able to have a look in an hour or so.'

'What do we do now, boss?' Gallagher asked.

'As soon as the tunnel's clear, you go straight to London. This time, do everything you have to to be sure you're not followed – if it takes all night. Tomorrow you start on-the-ground coverage of the buildings we've identified as the most likely hit sites. There are only three of you, which will make it tight, but we've got fifteen fixed OPs in operation. They'll need regular checking. They've got the "Joshua Reynolds", and they'll be told which are no longer relevant. If they're in doubt, they'll need one of you. It'll be a long, hard day and there may be no movement until Thursday. If there's anyone left from Sufuf Allah to make the hit, they may well lie low until that morning.'

'Who else is going to be on the lookout for these people?' Kelly asked.

'The DP Squad will be out in force, and Special Branch will have guns on the rooftops; I dare say a few dozen of Harry Cotterell's men, as well as MI5. But unless they've worked it out from Duckett's corpse at Aintree, I doubt if they've made a connection with Sufuf Allah yet – Duckett was English, and Andy removed his gun.' Bowring shrugged and went on. 'The one thing that could give them a lead is the fact that they know we're interested. I just hope to God the local police don't think of checking with Jones's unit in London.'

Kelly shook his head. 'They must have realized by now that something's going on. They know we've got a few soldiers in the country; we wouldn't be here unless there was work to be done.'

'That's my problem, so don't worry about that, Jack.'

'OK, but how the hell are three of us supposed to deal with a hit, even if we manage to find out where it's going to happen?'

'I'll be on the ground too, and James. And if we know where the hit's going to happen, it won't take a lot to stop it, you know that.'

'Aye,' Gallagher said. 'But how do we know what's going on?'

'Brenda will run central control. With all the radio traffic that'll be going on, you'll have to keep in contact by phone. James will issue you with mobiles, but use land lines where possible. Brenda . . . Miss MacFarlane will make her base at Londonderry

House, where she'll have three direct lines. Here are the numbers.' He handed each of them a slip of typed paper. 'Memorize and destroy.'

He looked at his small team – Kelly, Gallagher and Michelle. 'Personally I don't care too much about the money, but you might bear in mind that if His Holiness goes back to Rome unscathed, there's the thick end of thirty thousand dollars in it for each of you.'

13

Jim Mason went in Gallagher's car to London;
Kelly went with Michelle, who drove while the
Liverpudlian lounged in the passenger seat like a
man who'd overdone the cognac. 'If Bowring doesn't
care about the money, why the hell's he going through
with this?' he asked, mostly for the sake of talking.

'He hates to be beaten,' Michelle said.

'I suppose I knew that. But he doesn't seem
fanatical or anything. I mean, tonight, when we
almost blew the cover off HQ, he took it calmly
enough.'

'He has the same control over his anger as he has
over all his other emotions.'

'I suppose that's quite an attraction in a man,'
Kelly observed casually.

'It can be.'

They were driving east past Heathrow along the
A4. They had zigzagged across country from The
Hollies, and doubled back on themselves twice. They
had checked the car for bugs and were certain that
no other vehicle had stayed with them.

It was two hours since Bowring's briefing. The
tunnel had been cleared of the asphyxiating red
phosphorus and two more bodies. The face of one
of the bodies matched one of the two remaining
photographs in their gallery of mug shots.

Only Abdul abu Said remained unaccounted for. He seemed very much the sort of man who would take serious exception to having his plans interfered with by outside agencies. But looking for him in all the hundreds of places where he might choose to make his attack, among the hundreds of thousands of people who would be milling around the area of the Pope's route and rally seemed like a hell of a challenge.

'Basically, Bowring's plan's a bloody great punt,' Kelly said.

'You could say that every decision you take is a gamble. Bowring's way is to reduce the odds as much as he possibly can.'

'Well, he hasn't reduced them enough on this gig.'

It was around midnight when the SOS team checked into their rooms at Londonderry House. It had been a long day. When he was lying in his bed on the tenth storey of the hotel, it seemed to Kelly like a week since they had started tailing Duckett to Aintree that morning. But with well-trained will-power, he closed his eyes, emptied his mind of the day's events and the next day's doubts, and slept.

The wind had picked up during the night and dispersed the gloomy cover of cloud. The sun slanted mistily across Hyde Park at seven the following morning. Kelly ran the complete circumference of the park with his phone in one pocket and his Browning High Power in the other. As he neared the end of his run, the phone trilled. Miss MacFarlane sounded crisp.

'Good morning, Mr Kelly. All the observation posts are in operation. I'll be reporting to you regularly with all relevant sightings. You're to take the top end of Park Lane, from the Grosvenor House north.'

'OK, Miss M. Talk to you later,' he answered with a light-heartedness he didn't feel.

In his hotel, he changed into a well-cut, light-weight Italian suit and went back out into the hazy sunshine. He spent the next three hours prowling unopposed through the corridors of all the hotels, office blocks and apartment buildings that faced west across the park and into which he had cheerfully bluffed his way.

He checked every Middle Eastern face he saw – and there were many – but he hadn't forgotten Duckett, the fanatical white Muslim. At the same time, he was checking everywhere for any unusual signs – furtiveness, men carrying bulky, unlikely packages, anything that might have suggested preparation for attacking a hugely public figure with a security screen of several hundred men around him as he progressed in an armour-plated vehicle along the far side of the wide avenue.

It was a ridiculous brief, he thought to himself more than once, but those were Bowring's orders.

By two o'clock, he had seen nothing that seriously aroused his suspicions, and he was hungry. He ordered a sandwich in the lobby of one of the hotels, and used the time he took to eat it to watch everyone who came in and out. He was wiping the last crumbs from his mouth when someone he had not expected to see strolled in confidently but, in his white, open-neck shirt and tight Terylene trousers, quite out of place in this grand hotel.

The newcomer was also clearly taking note of everyone who crossed his line of vision. He spotted

Kelly before he had time to avoid it. He gave a slight smile and headed straight across the lofty hall and sat down in the chair beside him.

'Hello, boyo. What a surprise seeing you here.'

'Hello, Mick. Ditto. Are you chasing an African revolutionary on a recruitment drive or what?'

'Why, are you waiting to see him?' Mick Jones laughed. 'Course I'm not, Jack. I'm doing the same as you.'

'Are you? What's that, then?'

'Seeing what unsavoury characters are coming in and out. Have you finished your lunch, then?'

Kelly nodded and dropped a ten-pound note on the low table in front of him. 'That was a bloody expensive beef sandwich.'

'I'm sure Major Bowring will pay for it. Come on, let's take a walk. We may be able to help each other.'

On the wide, as yet uncrowded, pavement outside, they started to stroll northwards.

'I won't ask you directly what's going on,' Jones said. 'It wouldn't be fair and I don't suppose you'd tell me; anyway, I can guess. But you know, you may need help.'

Kelly grinned at him. 'We may. But I'm not going to ask for it.'

'All right, but you can tell Bowring. Look, I'm not interested in compromising whatever you're doing, but if you've got material information, you shouldn't be keeping it to yourselves. We know damn well the Sufuf Allah unit that came into the country hasn't left. Trouble is, they've dropped right out of sight, and it worries us.'

'Why, what do you think they might be up to?'

'For Christ's sake, Jack! Don't piss about,' the Welshman said with sudden sharpness. More conciliatory, he went on: 'You don't happen to know anything about somebody called Michael Duckett, do you?'

'Duckett?' Kelly shook his head. 'Doesn't sound very Islamic.'

'Well, he is. He goes by some Arab name now, or should I say, went. He was at the Papal rally in Liverpool yesterday and someone stuck a nine-inch blade into him.'

'Why would they do that?'

'To stop him taking a crack at the Pope, wouldn't you say?'

'You didn't say he had a gun on him.'

'Yeah, well, he didn't, but he has a record of disturbance at Islamic rallies and suchlike, and we'd had our eye on him as a possible fatwa merchant. One thing's for sure: he wasn't at that rally because he loves the Pope.'

'Well, he won't be causing any trouble tomorrow, will he, so you must be grateful to whoever neutralized him.'

'If only we knew who to be grateful to.'

'I'll let you know if I hear anything.'

'Look. If Bowring steps out of line tomorrow, and anything regrettable happens, there'll be trouble. As you can imagine we're not too keen on the privatization of the security services; not before our political masters decide it for us, anyway. I see you've got a mobile on you. Here's a number which will get me any time you want, all right? If you do, we may be able to overlook what's already been done.'

Kelly took a small piece of card on which Jones had scribbled a telephone number.

'OK, Mick. Now I'd better get on. I want to check the decorations up on Marble Arch.'

Jones shook his head. 'You've got my word, Jack. Contact me at the right time, and you're in the clear.'

'I'll remember that, Mick. Thanks.'

He gave the Welsh policeman a jovial nod, and extended his pace purposefully up Park Lane.

Mick was right, he thought, if anything went wrong, and SOS could be shown to have held back their intelligence from the security forces, of whichever branch, the faeces would hit the fan very hard.

He was crossing Upper Brook Street when his phone bleeped at him. It was Bowring.

'What's your position?'

Kelly told him.

'Are you on to anything?'

'Nothing hot.'

'Get yourself down to the Lanesborough, now.'

Bowring gave him a room number and cut off. Kelly, not too abruptly, turned around and began to stroll back down the other way, looking over his shoulder for a taxi. He got one before he'd walked twenty yards and was climbing out at the vast stucco building on Hyde Park Corner three minutes later.

Upstairs, in a fifth-floor room, he joined Bowring and two of his surveillance team. He introduced them briefly as John and Charlie. They looked like ex-policemen. Kelly wondered where Bowring had found them.

A telescope and camera with a 1000mm lens on tripods were pointing through the window that overlooked the constant whirlpool of traffic that spun round the triple arch of the Wellington Memorial. John sat on a chair with his eye glued to the telescope.

Newly developed black-and-white shots of a variety of individuals were clipped to a makeshift line to dry. Dozens more lay scattered on the double bed and dressing-table.

Bowring picked two up. 'Take a look at these,' he said, handing them to Kelly.

Kelly studied them for a few seconds, then nodded. 'You could be right. Can we blow them up more?'

'We're doing that right now. Is it ready yet, Charlie?'

'Give us another minute,' Charlie's voice came from the bathroom.

'Where was he, exactly?' Kelly asked.

'Over there, going into the front entrance of Apsley House with a crowd of other punters.'

'Was he with any of them?'

'Impossible to say, but he was the only Arab.'

'Here's the blow-up,' Charlie said carrying a dripping photograph from the bathroom which had become a temporary darkroom.

Bowring took it and laid it, still damp, on the bed.

From another stack of shots, he took one of the five which Harry Cotterell had given him ten days before and laid it beside the fresh one.

In the new shot – grainy from enlargement – a man was turning, looking around him, giving a three-quarter view of his heavy, dark features.

'Christ!' Kelly exclaimed, almost unwilling to believe that Bowring's strategy may have paid off. 'That's him.'

'Abdul abu Said,' Bowring said quietly. 'Yes. I think it is. And I doubt that he has more than a passing interest in the Duke of Wellington, if any.'

'That's the site, then,' Kelly said with a flurry of elation.

Bowring nodded his head, displaying no particular surprise that they had identified it. 'Not definitely, but probably. He may still be checking out the possibilities.' As he spoke, he picked up the phone beside the bed and punched out a number.

'Andy? Wherever you are, get down to Apsley House. Our last Joshua Reynolds went in about twenty minutes ago ... main public entrance. Get to it.'

He put the phone down. 'He's outside the Inn on the Park. You should see him in a minute, John.'

'Hang on!' John said, 'Our man's just come out!'

'Shit.' It was the first time Kelly had ever heard Bowring utter any kind of obscenity. 'Jack, get down there now. As soon as you're out of the building, I'll get you on the mobile and tell you which way he's gone.'

Kelly was out of the door before Bowring had finished the sentence. He almost sprinted down the deep-carpeted, silent corridor to the lifts, and clenched his fists with impatience as he waited the fifteen seconds it took for one of them to arrive and open its doors. It already contained a large, powerfully scented woman. Kelly grinned at her and hoped nobody else got in on the way down. To his frustration, the lift stopped again two floors down, and he calculated the advantage of getting out and finishing the descent by the stairs. He took a chance on the lift. It didn't stop again.

When the door opened on the ground floor he pushed past the later entrants and strode like an Olympic walker across the lobby to the main entrance on Hyde Park Corner.

He pulled his phone out and headed for the pedestrian tunnel leading to Hyde Park Corner tube station. As he reached the entrance, the phone trilled. He stopped and put it to his ear.

'Kelly?'

'Yeah.'

'He went down into the subway nearest Apsley House. Head for the ticket office.'

'Right.'

He stuffed the phone back in his pocket. It wouldn't be any use underground. He plunged down the stairs, trying not to push too many ambling tourists out of his way and followed the signs through the complex of tunnels to the booking hall. As he walked into it, he slowed to a sensible walk and headed for the ticket machines.

Abdul abu Said was there before him. Kelly hung back to put half a dozen people between them. He watched the self-service machine where the terrorist selected his ticket. He couldn't read the names from where he was, but when he reached it he punched the same destination – Tottenham Court Road – and hurried down to the eastbound platform.

When he got there, the platform was fairly full, but not so crowded that he couldn't see every person on it. Abdul abu Said wasn't among them.

Kelly did his best to disguise his panic as he looked

around him and tried to guess where the Palestinian had gone. He rushed through to the westbound platform, walked briskly along it, checking all the faces, fighting the urge to become frantic with frustration. The rush of wind that preceded the arrival of a train hit him with its musty smell. He moved to the back of the platform, to see if his quarry emerged from somewhere at the last minute; but Abdul abu Said didn't appear.

Kelly raced back to the other platform, where he could hear an eastbound train pulling in. He tried to take in all the people who surged towards the opening doors. No abu Said. Almost beside himself with despair, Kelly realized he'd lost the scent. He climbed back up the stairs, checking the interlinking passages as he went, but he knew the Palestinian had been following routine behaviour to throw off any possible surveillance, and he'd done it well.

Kelly emerged into the sunlight on the north side of Hyde Park Corner, and pulled out his phone again. He called one of Miss MacFarlane's numbers.

'I need to speak to the boss,' he said as soon as he heard her clear-cut voice in his ear. Without any preamble, she gave him a number which he stabbed angrily on the instrument.

Bowring answered.

'He lost me,' Kelly said bleakly.

There was a momentary pause before Bowring spoke. 'That's a great pity,' he said.

'It's a fucking disaster. I'm sorry, boss. He knew what he was doing.'

'Get back up here, then.'

'I'm sorry, boss,' Kelly said again when he was back

in the hotel bedroom that was now their *ad hoc* HQ. Gallagher, James and Michelle had arrived while he'd been running around the tunnels of the tube station.

'It's OK, Jack. These things happen. I should have got Andy down there sooner; two of you would have kept on to him.'

'Do you reckon he'll still go for it, then?'

'That's what he came here for. He'll have realized by now that he's lost the rest of his men and he's on his own.'

'Do you think those nine we took out yesterday were the whole of his unit, then?' Kelly asked.

'I wouldn't be surprised. In fact, the way things look, it's quite possible Abdul abu Said is the last active member of Sufuf Allah. If he wants to retain any credibility with his rivals back home, he's got to pull this thing off now. I would think too many people there know about it by now. And if there's no one left to do it for him, he'll have to do it himself.'

He was interrupted by Miss MacFarlane on the phone.

'Monsignor di Montefalco has been trying to reach you,' she said. 'Shall I put him through?'

'Yes, please.'

The cleric was on the phone himself a few seconds later.

'Major Bowring?'

'Yes, Monsignor?'

'What has happened?' Montefalco sounded agitated. 'We have been informed, somewhat reluctantly, by your MI5 that an English Muslim was killed at the Papal Mass at Aintree. They thought he may have been there to make an attempt on His Holiness's life.'

'Yes, Monsignor. We know all about that.'

'You do?'

'We knew about it four hours before they did.'

'Thank God.' The priest sounded relieved. 'Did a man called Father Sullivan come and see you?'

'Yes.'

'Did you do as he asked?'

'No. We're still attending to the matter.'

'That is what I hoped. I am most grateful to you. There has been some ... confusion. I can't explain now.'

'I understand.'

'And I may be sure you are continuing with the job?'

'You may, Monsignor.'

'Do we still have cause to be concerned?'

'You had, but we have the situation well under control.'

'That is good news. If you need me, you will be able to contact me at the nunciate until tomorrow morning. After that I shall be accompanying His Holiness to Hyde Park. I pray that you will be successful.'

'So do I, Monsignor, though I dare say to less effect.'

'Thank you, Major. And God bless you.'

Bowring put the phone down with a grin. 'We have a blessing straight from the Vatican; that should do the trick,' he said. 'But I suppose we'd better make plans as well.'

With a swing in her stride and a camera fitted with a

zoom lens over her shoulder, Michelle walked through the doors of 'Number One, London', Apsley House – the London home of the Dukes of Wellington since it was built by the first of that line in the 1820s.

The staterooms and the fine collections of pictures, tapestries and Wellington militaria were all open to the public that day. Michelle found herself going in with a party of French tourists who seemed happy to absorb her into their group. She bought every guide to the place that might contain plans or information, and photographed the staircases and the wide, open corridors.

On the first floor, as the other sightseers were engaged in more innocent research, she spotted a door marked 'Private', tried the handle, found it open and slipped through. She was ready with an explanation in rudimentary English, that she was looking for a lavatory.

But in the surprising hush of the private quarters, there was no one to challenge her. She flitted along the passage on the other side of the door until she found what she was looking for: a flight of stairs up to the next floor.

While Michelle was inside the house, Charlie, the more competent photographer of the surveillance team, was photographing the south, east and north elevations from the outside. More specifically, he was trying to identify and capture on film the most suitable windows, or other apertures for aiming and firing some kind of ballistic device at the centrepiece of the Papal motorcade.

Kelly and Gallagher made as thorough a survey as they could to assess the ranges and the weapon most likely to be used, approaching the task, as they had done all along, as if they had been granted the contract to shoot the Pope themselves.

Back in the Lanesborough, Michelle gave them her findings – an approximate, incomplete plan of the first and second storeys of the building. She'd been interrupted early in her search, and bluffed her way out, but hadn't found another opportunity to carry on. She'd had to guess at the dimensions and exact positions of the private rooms, but with the help of Charlie's external research they were able to put together a working diagram of the house.

'Not quite as much information as we had for the Iran Embassy siege, but then it's a much smaller job,' Bowring observed.

Kelly and Gallagher presented Bowring with the consensus of their opinions.

'If the guy knows what he's doing,' the Scot said, 'he'll use some kind of rocket – a Carl Gustav, maybe, or if they're using old Soviet weapons, an RPG7.'

Bowring shook his head. 'Too bulky to get in and too much blow-back. Unless he was in a sixty-foot gallery, the risk of setting fire to the place would be too high.'

'But he's not going to give a bugger about burning the place down, is he?' Gallagher argued.

'Yes, he is. I'd say that Abdul abu Said is far too interested in staying alive so he can wield his bit of power to risk either getting caught or fried alive. Why don't you think he'd use a simple high-power rifle? A 7.62 round would pierce the Pope-mobile without too much trouble.'

'No, boss,' Kelly said. 'He'd only have the one shot, and a bloody tricky shot. It might penetrate the glass, but the chances are it would get deflected.

What about an American 66mm rocket – an M66? Less blow-back and breaks down into two pieces, maybe three foot each.'

Bowring thought for a moment. 'I agree,' he said. 'Of the options available, I think that's what I'd choose. However, we're not certain that Apsley House is the hit site. Our friend may have just been making a recce, choosing his spot, and there are other possible sites. I'm keeping all observation posts in operation while we concentrate on this one. But you're going to have to be ready for a complete change of venue. At least our surveillance know exactly what they're looking for.'

'So we get back on the streets, then?' Kelly asked.

'That's right. You take the tube station. James, take the subway exit by Apsley House. Andy, you cover the bottom of Park Lane. Michelle, you stay up here and help John and Charlie. Abu Said's not going to be able to do anything after the place closes, so you can come off then, but I want you all out again tomorrow from seven onwards, and remember, there'll be a lot of other people out there watching, so make sure they don't pick you up.'

Kelly flopped on to his bed at ten that night. He was deciding whether or not he really wanted to watch the next film that was being broadcast on the movie channel when he heard a knock on his door.

Instantly, he was on his guard. He got up silently, picked up his Browning and shoved the holster under the bed with his foot. He walked across the room without a sound and stood with his back to the wall, a few feet from the opening side of the door. He reached across and released the lock.

The person outside knocked again.

'Come in,' he said sleepily, directing his voice into the corner.

The door handle turned and the door swung open. No one came in. Kelly's nerves tingled: he prepared himself and lifted his gun a little higher. He held his breath, one, two, three, four, five seconds.

Michelle walked in.

'It's only me,' she said, turning to him with a smile as he stared at her along the barrel of his gun.

'Why didn't you ring me and tell me you were coming?' Kelly said, breathing freely once again.

'I just decided, as I was walking past your room. You don't mind, do you?'

'Not much.'

She closed the door behind her. 'I didn't feel like watching the television and I don't think I'll get to sleep too easily.'

'Too much excitement for you?'

'Probably.'

'Do you want a drink, then?'

'Not really.'

'I do,' Kelly said and walked to the fridge in the corner of the room, opened it and poured himself a large whisky.

'Sit down,' he said, waving at one of the two armchairs, then sat himself in the other. 'What do you want, then?'

She raised her shoulders. 'I don't know really; maybe just to know what to expect tomorrow.'

Kelly grunted. 'That's anybody's guess. Trouble is, we haven't got a clue how many we're up against.'

'It can't be many, if abu Said is making the preparations himself. He didn't let himself be in the firing line at Summerfold.'

'We don't know that, not for sure. But it's all right, I don't think he's got anyone with him either.' He put his feet on the glass coffee table between them and took a long slug of his drink. 'I just wish I knew for certain, because if we do find out where and when he's going to make his hit, when we go in we won't have time to look over our shoulders. Is that what's worrying you?'

She shook her head. 'No. I just don't want to mess it up, that's all.'

'Well, if you do, you won't be around to regret it, so what's the worry?' Kelly said, throwing his hand in the air. 'But look,' he said, more gently, remembering well the times before his first operations with the SAS, 'I know what it's like, and to tell you the truth, there's no advice I can give you. You just get used to it. Come on, have one big drink, then go to bed.'

She gave him a long, slightly quizzical look and abruptly stood up. 'No thanks. I don't need a drink. I'll watch a movie.'

'Do you want to watch it with me?'

She smiled down at him. 'Not yet. Maybe another time. Thanks for talking to me.' She walked to the door. 'See you in the morning.'

'Yeah, sure,' Kelly said without moving in his chair. He watched her leave, and give him a last quick smile before she closed the door and was gone.

Maybe another time. Kelly shook his head and switched on the television.

Thursday morning, the morning of the last day of

Pope John Paul II's visit to Britain, dawned lightly swathed in a veil of mist. There was a definite chill to the air as Kelly and Michelle met up to jog along Rotten Row.

'OK?' he asked her.

'Sure.'

She looked it. There was not a hint of nervousness as she ran beside him with her hair flowing behind her.

The park was already busy at a quarter to seven with other runners and riders and a string of black Household Cavalry horses returning from exercise. In the top corner of the park, a few dozen men were making final adjustments to the stage and equipment that would be used for the open-air mass scheduled to begin at eleven o'clock which a hundred thousand people were expected to attend.

To reach it, the Pope's motorcade from Westminster would be passing around Hyde Park Corner at ten-thirty.

'There's not a lot we can do until Apsley House opens at nine,' Kelly said. 'But we may as well stay in our track-suits and watch for an hour until Andy and James replace us.'

They sat, like a pair of lovers who had spent the night together, on a bench a hundred yards from Apsley House. As they watched, they talked not about the day in front of them, but about Kelly's past, his experiences in the desert campaign, in Ireland and the Falklands, which helped to put into perspective the risks they might face in a few hours' time.

Bowring telephoned soon after seven to check that they were in place. He could see them from where he was, he said, so could the OP in the Intercontinental.

Reassured by this, Kelly and Michelle settled down for a few more hours of waiting.

14

Three hours later, Kelly was beginning to sweat. The mist had cleared to uncover a strong sun, but it was lack of information, not heat, that was causing his discomfort.

They had seen nothing. The OPs had reported nothing. Even Bowring in his regular progress calls was starting to sound irritable.

Kelly, changed now from his track-suit into jeans and denim jacket, was sitting on the bench while Michelle was jogging round the block where Apsley House stood. He glanced up from his *Daily Telegraph* to look west along Knightsbridge for the hundredth time to see if anyone of interest was approaching from that direction. Since before nine o'clock there had been a steady stream of pedestrian tourists and people coming to the Papal Mass. Most turned through the gate into the park before they reached him.

He spotted the bulky figure from fifty yards – a very stout Arab in a spotless, creamy-white djellaba, walking slowly, with the air of a man who suffered from his own self-inflicted burden. Of medium height, heavily bearded, wearing dark glasses and with a black-and-white checked *shemagh* swathing his head, he didn't turn into the park but waddled on up towards the corner.

Kelly was reading his paper as the Arab passed by

without looking at him. He waited a few moments before he stood up and walked through the gate among a steady stream of the Pope's followers, out of sight of the bulky figure. He pulled out his phone and called Bowring at the Lanesborough.

'Have you clocked a very fat Arab, passing opposite you about now?'

'Yes. We've got him. He's gone on past Apsley.'

Kelly felt a stab of disappointment. 'There's something not right about the way he's moving.'

'We've already photographed him. We'll check him out. The motorcade is passing Buckingham Palace now,' he added tightly. 'Should be with you in about ten minutes. Hang on! He's turning back! Michelle's just come round from the other side. I think she's on to him.'

'Right,' Kelly said, turning back towards Knightsbridge. 'I'm on my way.'

'Good luck, Jack.'

Kelly moved as fast as he could without breaking into a run. He was just in time to see the Arab join a short queue of tourists going into Apsley House. Michelle was a few yards behind.

He could hear the cheering now as the Papal motorcade progressed slowly up Constitution Hill. The Arab had disappeared though the doorway of the house, followed by Michelle. He couldn't see Gallagher or James. He broke into a run, dodging and weaving through the dawdling pedestrians to the great wrought-iron gates. He sprinted now up the steps to the main door, but before he got there, his way was blocked by a commissionaire and a uniformed police constable.

'What's the hurry?' said the policeman.

Kelly couldn't risk an argument or a scene.

'Special forces,' he said crisply. 'I've got to get in there, quick.'

'ID?'

'Of course I'm not carrying ID.'

The policeman and commissionaire, joined by another, moved to more effectively stop Kelly entering as a small tail-back of sightseers built up. He was ready to burst with frustration. 'Listen, you arseholes, this is bloody vital.' He had a sudden inspiration, and pulled his phone from his pocket and punched the number Mick Jones had given him.

His fists clenched and unclenched as he waited ten rings for the call to be answered.

'Jones,' Kelly heard with a surge of relief.

'Mick. Jack. I've got to get into Apsley House. I've got a copper barring the way.'

'Tell him to radio central control right now.'

Kelly looked at the immutable constable. 'Call your control – now,' he snapped.

The policeman doubtfully clicked on the radio on his lapel. 'Control. B157 at Apsley House. There's a character come rushing up, wants to go in.' He waited and listened for fifteen nerve-shredding seconds, watching Kelly all the while.

'What's your name?' he asked him at last.

'Kelly.'

'Last rank and regiment?'

'Sergeant, 22 SAS.'

The policeman stepped aside.

Kelly ran in, up the first flight of stairs, looking around him for the Arab or Michelle.

On the first floor, he sprinted to the door at the end of the gallery which Michelle had told them about in her briefing the evening before. He went through into the relative calm on the other side. Again there was no one about. He listened but heard nothing to tell him if Michelle and the Arab had come that way. He looked for the stairs up to the next storey, found them without meeting anyone else and ran up.

On the second floor he had to take a gamble. He weighed up the options and headed east; that was where the closest shot could be taken. Then he saw Michelle. She had her Browning drawn and was standing with her back against the wall beside a door at the end of a wide corridor.

He stopped five yards short of the door and beckoned her to him. She reached him in a few silent strides. He put his mouth to her ear.

'What's the story?'

'He's gone in and managed to lock the door.'

'Does he know you saw him?'

'No. I hadn't reached the top of the stairs when he went in.'

'I hope you're bloody right. Let's go.'

Kelly walked along the soft, sound-deadening carpet until he was three feet from the door. He lifted his right leg, bending his knee, brought it back and powered his heel into the lock set in heavy mahogany.

It cracked, but the door was still in place. He gritted his teeth, aware that he'd already blown fifty per cent of their chances, lifted his leg again and with the desperate strength which that knowledge gave him, smashed his heel at the splintered lock once more.

The door shuddered open with the impact.

Kelly and Michelle sprang to each side of it. Kelly raised a hand for her to wait until he gave a sign. Gripping their Brownings in both hands, they spun round together and crouched in the doorway.

The Arab had his back to an open window, where a curtain flapped in the breeze and the noise of the Pope's approach was rising in a crescendo.

He had shed his bulk and his djellaba, and was facing them now with pure hatred on his face and a loaded M66 rocket-launcher on his shoulder.

Twelve silenced shots spat from both Brownings. The rocket-launcher crashed to the ground. The Arab's dark bearded face seemed to disintegrate and the ravaged T-shirt he wore turned crimson as he stumbled back and collapsed to lie with sightless eyes gazing at the fine plasterwork of the ceiling.

Kelly ran into the room and placed two more, needless 9mm rounds in the mangled, bloody mess of the Arab's torso. He reached down beside the dead man and deactivated the rocket-launcher.

Michelle had followed Kelly into the room. She was by the window watching the Pope-mobile and its squadron of motorcycle outriders pass at ten miles an hour between Apsley House and the hotel opposite. She turned and looked down at the man whose brains she had just blown out. Unconsciously, she made a sign of the cross.

The sound of running up the stairs and several heavy sets of feet pounding towards them echoed down the corridor.

Mick Jones burst into the room, followed by Bowring and two plain-clothes policemen, all with weapons drawn.

They stopped inside the splintered door.

'Shit!' Jones hissed. Kelly didn't miss the sweat that was pouring off the Welshman's forehead.

'Close the door,' Bowring snapped at one of the policemen, who obeyed without question.

Jones turned to Bowring. 'Christ, you cut that fine. You're bloody lucky you got to him.'

'So are you, Mick,' Bowring said more calmly. 'Because if we hadn't, your people certainly wouldn't have. How did you know he was here?'

'I told him,' Kelly owned up.

Bowring looked at Jones. 'There you are. Nobody could call us uncooperative. And what's more, we're going to quietly slip away from here while you and your men take all the credit for saving the Pope's life and deflecting some nasty repercussions in the Middle East peace talks. I wouldn't be surprised if you got a nice gong for it.'

A policeman now, but always at heart a member of the Regiment, Jones looked at his old squadron commander. 'You always were a jammy bugger, boss.'

Bowring looked back at him and nodded slowly with a faint smile. 'And don't you forget it.' He turned to Kelly and Michelle. 'Right, let's get out of here.'

For once, Piers Bowring looked as though he was enjoying one of his own dinner parties at Summerfold House that evening. The only outsider to join the SOS team at table was Harry Cotterell from MI6 – a gesture of appeasement on Bowring's part.

'I suppose we ought to be grateful to you,' Cotterell said. 'You seem to have wiped out the whole of Sufuf Allah in the last three days.'

'I hope so. They were a particularly nasty bunch.'

'But Piers, we can't let this kind of thing happen.

You should have brought our people in and let them deal with it.'

'Stop fussing,' Bowring said lightly. 'His Holiness is going home intact. As far as those who are aware of what happened are concerned, the AT Squad were responsible. Where's the problem?'

'We've still got the small matter of a Palestinian shot in the streets of West London, and an English Muslim stabbed to death at Aintree.'

'Sorry, Harry. Can't help you there.'

Cotterell shook his head, resigned. 'What have you done with the rest of them?'

Bowring looked at James, who was bringing in bottles of calvados, port and brandy. 'James?'

'All gone, sir,' the butler said curtly.

'We do have some photographs for you, though,' said Bowring. 'But we won't look at them now. They're not a pretty sight.'

'Did you lose anyone?'

'I can't tell you that, Harry.'

'Look, Piers. Of course, you know that it would be too messy for me to start making a fuss about this, but for God's sake, please don't take on any more jobs inside the UK.'

'That I'm happy to agree to. I found it very disagreeable to have my privacy here threatened. No more operations in Britain, I promise.'

'I'll drink to that,' Cotterell replied. 'But I'm amazed anyone from Sufuf Allah found their way here, with the precautions you take.'

A look of annoyance passed across Bowring's face. 'There was what you might call a minor cock-up with a major result. Somewhere, perhaps when they stopped outside Oxford, a bug was put on Miss

MacFarlane's car. No one checked when they left to come here – James found it later that evening before he and Andy went to London.' He lifted an eyebrow. 'It would have been a doddle for them after that, and Miss MacFarlane's was the only car that actually came back to the house.'

Cotterell nodded, glancing round the room. 'And am I right in thinking there's one less of you than there was?'

There was a moment's silence in the room. No one wanted to admit to an outsider what had happened to Terry Haynes. At the same time, to deny his existence and the part he had played in the eradication of the small but deadly Sufuf Allah seemed disloyal to the memory of the gutsy little cockney.

Bowring picked up his team's mood and nodded. 'Yes. We did lose a man, a very useful soldier, and a good man. He's quite a loss to us.' He sighed. 'But there it is. He knew the risks of working in an operation like this; we all do and we've all learnt to live with it; otherwise we wouldn't be here.'

Bowring met Monsignor di Montefalco at Dowson's house in Lord North Street next morning.

'Major, I should like to thank you. The security services here informed us last night that they had found and neutralized a serious threat to His Holiness's safety.' The cleric paused. 'I got the impression that they were slightly embarrassed about it.'

'They'll get over it, Monsignor. We didn't tell them until the job was done, as per our terms of engagement with you.'

'I understand. The contract will be honoured. I'm

also grateful that you chose not to act on the instructions of Father Sullivan and, er, Cardinal O'Keane.'

Bowring looked at Montefalco with a smile in his still, grey eyes. 'If you tell me what's going to happen to O'Keane now, I'll take you to lunch at Greens.'

Montefalco struggled for a moment. 'Well, it will be a matter of public record soon. He is retiring from active ministry, going back to Chicago.' He shrugged his narrow shoulders. 'Better than a South American posting, anyway,' he said fastidiously.

While Bowring and the monsignor talked in London, Kelly woke up in his room at The Hollies. The sun was streaming in through the windows and a light breeze wafted in the scents and sounds of the woodland beyond the neat Victorian garden.

He heard a soft step on the stairs and glanced across the bed to the door. Michelle, in a flimsy dressing-gown and with her hair tumbling in disarray over her shoulders, came in with two large French cups of coffee. She put them on a table beside the bed, and climbed under the duvet beside Kelly.

He put out a hand and ran it through her hair, then allowed it to wander down to her breasts.

'What made you change your mind?' he said quietly.

'Does it matter?' she answered.

'Not much, but I'd still like to know.'

She bent down and kissed his battered face and stroked his chest with a hand which, slowly, tantalizingly, slipped down to touch his tight-muscled stomach, his thighs and burgeoning erection. 'I'll tell you later,' she murmured between kisses.

*   *   *

A long, blissful while later, he asked her again.

'I slept with you,' she said slowly, 'because the Boss said you deserved it.'

Kelly tightened up, ready to protest.

She calmed him with a caress of her long, gentle fingers. 'And because he said it would do me a lot of good.' She smiled serenely. 'And do you know something? He was absolutely right.'

OTHER TITLES IN SERIES FROM 22 BOOKS

Available now at newsagents and booksellers
or use the order form opposite

SOLDIER A SAS: Behind Iraqi Lines
SOLDIER B SAS: Heroes of the South Atlantic
SOLDIER C SAS: Secret War in Arabia
SOLDIER D SAS: The Colombian Cocaine War
SOLDIER E SAS: Sniper Fire in Belfast
SOLDIER F SAS: Guerrillas in the Jungle
SOLDIER G SAS: The Desert Raiders
SOLDIER H SAS: The Headhunters of Borneo
SOLDIER I SAS: Eighteen Years in the Elite Force
SOLDIER J SAS: Counter-insurgency in Aden
SOLDIER K SAS: Mission to Argentina
SOLDIER L SAS: The Embassy Siege
SOLDIER M SAS: Invisible Enemy in Kazakhstan
SOLDIER N SAS: The Gambian Bluff
SOLDIER O SAS: The Bosnian Inferno
SOLDIER P SAS: Night Fighters in France

*   *   *   *   *

SOLDIER OF FORTUNE 1:   Valin's Raiders
SOLDIER OF FORTUNE 2:   The Korean Contract
SOLDIER OF FORTUNE 4:   Operation Nicaragua

All at £4.99 net

22 Books offers an exciting list of titles in these series. All the books are available from:

Little, Brown and Company (UK) Limited,
PO Box 11,
Falmouth,
Cornwall TR10 9EN.

Alternatively you may fax your order to the above address.
Fax number: 0326 376423.

Payments can be made by cheque or postal order (payable to Little, Brown and Company) or by credit card (Visa/Access). Do not send cash or currency. UK customers and BFPO please allow £1.00 for postage and packing for the first book, plus 50p for the second book, plus 30p for each additional book up to a maximum charge of £3.00 (seven books or more). Overseas customers, including customers in Ireland, please allow £2.00 for the first book, plus £1.00 for the second book, plus 50p for each additional book.

NAME (BLOCK LETTERS PLEASE) ....

....

ADDRESS ....

....

....

☐ I enclose my remittance for £_____

☐ I wish to pay by Access/Visa

Card number
☐☐☐☐☐ ☐☐☐☐ ☐☐☐☐ ☐☐☐☐

Card expiry date
☐☐ ☐☐